Crisis Marketing:

when bad things
happen to
good companies

3RD EDITION

Joe Marconi

Also by Joe Marconi

Getting the Best from Your Ad Agency (1991)

Crisis Marketing (1992)

Beyond Branding (1993)

Image Marketing (199)

Shock Marketing (1997)

Crisis Marketing (Revised, 2nd edition, 1997)

The Complete Guide to Publicity (1999)

The Brand Marketing Book (2000)

Future Marketing (2001)

Reputation Marketing (2002)

Cause Marketing (2002)

Public Relations: The Complete Guide (2004)

Creating the Marketing Experience (2005)

The Writing Book (2008)

Crisis Marketing:

when bad things
happen to
good companies

3RD EDITION

Joe Marconi

Crisis Marketing
3rd Edition

ISBN: 978-0-9819095-1-6
© 2008 Joe Marconi

Cover Design: Gregory S. Paus

Published by
Dickens~Webster
Publishing
A division of
Bruce Bendinger Creative Communications, Inc.
• 2144 N. Hudson • Chicago, IL 60614 •
• TEL: 773-871-1179 • FAX: 773-281-4643 •
dickenswebster@gmail.com

Dickens~Webster
Publishing

For Todd and Kristin and Emily

Contents

Preface to the Third Edition

Marketing once largely focused on matters of pricing and distribution and was much more of a *sales*-oriented process and less about *communications*. That's no longer the case.

Modern marketing is the umbrella term covering packaging, promotions, and positioning, under which are advertising, public relations, sales, research, shareholder communications, philanthropy, sponsorships, as well as pricing and distribution. Marketing must also work closely with other departments in an organization, including the legal department, particularly in matters relating to the subject of this book.

The idea that marketing and legal would work closely on anything other than grudgingly getting submitted ad copy approved is, for marketers, a frightening thought. The reasoning is that marketers typically want to go to ever greater lengths and do whatever Is necessary to be innovative, creative and aggressively competitive, while lawyers are generally more conservative and are inclined to reign-in bold, aggressive, edgy activity, staying well inside the lines of caution. That's a generalization, but it's also been the reality of marketers for decades.

But today business is different, being more globally-focused In many Instances, and people are more litigious, especially in the United States, making the sometimes uncomfortable teaming of lawyers with marketers – and its attendant clash of cultures – an awkward fact of life.

Crisis Marketing is about such changes in the way businesses and organizations have had to reposition themselves and rethink their policies and practices.

This book emphasizes the importance of a well-crafted marketing plan, specifically as it can be applied to crisis marketing, the term used to describe strategies and tactics for sustaining successful marketing programs before, during, and after stakeholders and the public learn of – and react to – personal or business situations that find a company "under fire" and struggling to save its business, its customers and its reputation.

By anticipating potential crises, if only with relatively broad contingency planning, laying a foundation on which to build a more defined reactive position, a troubling situation may well be limited or, perhaps, averted altogether.

Crisis Marketing is not only a corrective measure or a disaster plan, it is an outline for "how to keep the disaster alarm from going off, but what to do if it does" strategy.

Is crisis marketing different from crisis management?
For purposes of this discussion, there is no difference.

In actual common practice, however, the differences could be substantial. The term "crisis management" means literally *managing or coping with a crisis situation*, not regarding the problem as a long-term matter. Anything more requires both the attention of, and a commitment from, senior management. A response to a crisis should not be solely the province of the PR or legal department. Everyone, at all levels throughout the company or organization needs to be briefed and be part of a total response if disaster is to be avoided and success is to be achieved.

Crisis Marketing was first published in 1991 with a revised updated edition in 1997. In the time since then, to use a past tense of an already overworked phrase, *the more things changed, the more they stayed the same*. The public and businesses are surprised not at all to learn of companies in trouble, for a variety reasons, on an almost daily basis.

In the 21st century, no one appears shocked at revelations that businesses have cut corners to save money and by doing so might have put segments of the public at risk.

Bad behavior, bad decisions, and outright corruption are no longer surprising in business since the bottom fell out of Enron, Global Crossing, and Worldcom-MCI, to name just three. It's removed the element of surprise from bad news.

Moreover, the public has become very familiar with the corporate PR responses – the denials and righteous indignation, followed by apologies, tears, and a scramble to shift blame and responsibility elsewhere.

Dealing with a business or organizational crisis at virtually every stage is reflected in the most significant ways to matters of *public relations, branding, reputation* and overall *image.*

From the beginning, this book was very well received *internationally. Crisis Marketing* was thought in 1991 by marketers and students of marketing, to be a very timely subject. During the time it took to write the book – and its subsequent updated second edition in 1997 and for several years after – comments and reviews would note the timeliness of the need for a useful, readable book on crisis management. As I write these words, it is nearly 20 years since the first edition and, only yesterday, a university colleague referred to the timeliness of my writing on crisis management. Clearly, crises in business will always be a timely subject and are now considered as usual a concern as filing the company's quarterly tax return. But however usual business crises may be, their impact on people, places and things can be enormous.

Today fads and trends, digital technology, and the seemingly constant drum-beating for "new and improved" versions of products are a fact of marketing life, so are businesses in trouble.

And much of the public has become cynical regarding crisis management practices, having witnessed too many tearful CEOs and elected officials, community leaders, sports heroes, entertainers, and private citizens' public responses that all seem to be following a similar script after being caught (or caught up) in disturbing, compromising, scandalous, usually Illegal situations.

Public apologies are common in segments of evening news programs. Embattled executives go on the offensive to sidestep responsibility for wrongdoing on their watch, then often agree to put an end to the crises by simply, quietly going away in exchange for huge amounts of money, which causes the public to become even more cynical of the process.

The basic nature of business crises may not have changed much over 20 years, but responses and reactions have stretched from plausible to petulant to preposterous to pathetic. And not curiously, many of the principals In crisis situations Immediately get representation to secure lucrative book deals and speaking engagements. No wonder the public Is cynical.

A crisis might come in the form of an Internet rumor or a predatory competitor, or result from a natural disaster or a scandal. Considering some of the "classic" business crises – the Exxon Valdez oil spill, Tylenol's deadly product-tampering case, as well as assorted CEO misallocation of company funds, a multitude of scams, and sex in the executive suite – who would have thought it would be high winds and water that would threaten to destroy the economy of cities and states, and inflict such severe damage on entire nations.

The effects of the 2004 tsunami on areas in Indonesia, Thailand and Nicobar Island in India, as well as Hurricane Katrina on Louisiana and Mississippi in the U.S. in 2005, Hurricane Ike on Cuba and several American cities, most notably Galveston and Houston in Texas in 2008, quakes, floods, fires, and assorted other natural disasters, nearly devastating parts of the world. Commercial and residential buildings were left with shaken foundations and severely damaged confidence in those who were supposed to provide protection.

Sometimes leaders see a disaster coming and take preventative steps to avert it. Sometimes they see it and take no action at all. And sometimes, there is simply not enough time to prepare and protect. Anticipating worst case situations and taking precautions must become the new way of doing business as usual.

A brief word of caution: this work presumes innocence. That is to say, a company correctly charged with dumping toxic waste can ask forgiveness of regulators, customers and the general public and offer to make restitution. The company can't, however, convince even a naive constituency that the practice was somehow all right just because the company or its management or spokespersons insist they're really nice guys.

A Wall Street "inside trader" took poor kids to a baseball game as a way of saying to the public (and to the judge) that, despite the mega-millions he pocketed on shady deals, he really wasn't such a bad guy. Uh-huh. The stunt was such a transparently manipulative attempt at an ill-conceived public relations move that no one, including the judge and the public, was impressed. But it did send a message about the faultiness of packaged crisis management practices. Indicted felons have suddenly become born-again and receive a spiritual awakening immediately before going to trial, and individuals caught betraying a public trust tearfully reveal humbling histories of addiction to painkillers, alcohol, and more. Others just blame all their missteps, chicanery, and screw-ups on "the media." Those folks won't find many helpful tips in this book.

Rather, *Crisis Marketing* examines ethical companies, industries, and professions that unjustly come under fire.

The drug laboratories, chicken farmers, and even fast-food restaurants are the faces of evil incarnate, or are they victims of self-serving special interests and pressure groups? What can they do? What *should* they do?

The most successful salespeople think of challenging situations not as problems guaranteed to sink the company ship, but as opportunities – something like "making lemonade out of life's lemons." Simplistic or not, experienced marketers understand the importance of not giving up too early.

As a first step it's important to get focused. Whether you view your issue as a crisis, a challenge, or an opportunity might determine if you'll get a chance to take a second step. Without pretending it's always easy (it's not), this book is intended to help leaders and students chart ways out of bad times.

For contributions, assistance, encouragement, and support, thanks to Francesca Van Gorp at the American Marketing Association, Rick Ronvik, Viki King, Terry Erdmann, Paula Block, and the usual suspects: Rich Girod, Lonny Bernardi and Guy Kendler. Special thanks also to editor/publisher/friend Bruce Bendinger and the A-team at Bendinger-Davis' newest imprint, Dickens-Webster Publishing.

And to Karin Gottschalk Marconi whose contributions to my work could fill books themselves.

Joe Marconi
Chicago, Illinois
October, 2008

Special Supplement
for the 3rd Edition

The Global Challenge for Crisis Marketing

The Global Challenge for Crisis Marketing

Going Bigger, Wider, Faster and Farther— for Better or Worse

In 2008 the mantra of candidates seeking the U.S. presidency was *change*. It's a word that, while highly unspecific, says a lot. More importantly, it's a word people can read a great deal into, both good and bad, though most people believe when they hear "a change is gonna come" it's a sign of positive changes on the way.

Few words describe marketing as well as *change*. Even when not ushering in a new century or celebrating an event worth commemorating, a desire for change is present in people's everyday lives... every day. A faster car; a computer that can do even more and do it better and cheaper; a healthier, trimmer figure; a new hairstyle; new colors; a new look; new ideas; the ability to communicate around the world—and into space and back again— it's change that drives us, motivates us and fuels our dreams. It's the newest idea, the latest product or brand, a new line extension, an acquisition or a merger or spin-off, a redesign of packaging, a switch in manufacturing systems, or the finalizing of licensing agreements. Or something else. Change is essential for a business to maintain its freshness and its market share. As competition becomes more aggressive and intense on an international scale, changes are often necessary.

And thanks to advanced—and ever-advancing—technology, very small companies and organizations can do business internationally and appear on web pages and sites to be on a par with much larger, more established companies and, at the same time, should they choose to do so, global giants can personalize contacts and messages to offer service reflecting what people like most about dealing with smaller companies.

Change can be rapid or gradual. Research and Development efforts can and might take years of quietly working behind the scenes, testing, refining and creating something new, special, or uniquely different—something that, by its look, package, presentation, cost, placement, or use may reflect a broad change in the market or in public opinion, tastes and trends—possibly, a revolution—*changing* the way people think about a subject or even how they do what they do. And it can all happen at once, around the world, on as large or small a scale as circumstances or the marketing plan define.

... and now the bad news

Unfortunately for marketers, *not all* change is good—especially in an era where some agencies and consultancies make it a practice to attack and undermine corporate competitors, using negative ads and damaging viral marketing campaigns—word-of-mouth information.

And technology has made egregious conduct and unethical practices much easier, faster and less costly to accomplish.

Simply stated, sometimes bad things happen to good companies.

In business, ethical practices should be the order of the day and not even need to be mentioned. But some companies make significant advances by aggressively "going after" their competition—not with lower prices, higher quality, better service or superior guarantees, but by attacking them with rumors, ridicule and disparaging references in ads and anecdotes that stay barely inside the legal limits. Often, in modern business, crises are created deliberately. And quickly.

It only takes a word or two to make or break a company. Some 50 years ago John F. Kennedy told an interviewer that he liked to unwind by reading the English writer Ian Fleming's spy novels. That one comment in a major publication launched a worldwide interest that became a phenomenon, continuing to be a multimillion-dollar book, film and merchandise franchise, and making Fleming's creation of James Bond and "Agent 007", the most famous impeccably tailored, quick-witted, martini-drinking playboy spy in the world.

Similarly, the most random negative comment by a prominent or influential person can put a product or company on shaky ground and create declines in sales, profits and bad reputation.

Unfortunately for businesses, some changes occur outside of the research labs and outside of their control. Well laid plans can be stopped cold or sent veering into unanticipated directions, bringing a dramatic shift in the marketing landscape in ways not welcomed by business or consumers.

Small problems, minor oversights, a moment of laxity can become a crisis.

A business or corporate crisis, as with a personal crisis, is a relative matter, smaller or larger in scope than some perceive and possibly only of concern to those most closely affected by it.

Technology has allowed many small and mid-size businesses operate on a global scale, making what might be minor problems visible to larger audiences, thus more widely exposed and vulnerable to instances of misinformation, misinterpretation and misunderstanding.

Businesses welcome advances that permit requests for information or orders placed for products or services in New York City to be easily met with a response—and possible new business relationships—from Chicago, Berlin, Johannesburg or Hong Kong. A small business today can relatively inexpensively serve customers and clients around the world by simply pressing a few keys on a desktop, notebook or handheld computer. Opportunities abound. International communication, information and commerce are fast and easy, with many organizations doing much more with much less, and in many more places.

So marketing for large companies or small businesses is global—or *can be* global—with only a desire for it to be so, and an Internet connection. But just as the opportunities for success are greater and more easily and economically available, real or potential problems can surface and become crisis situations getting worldwide notice every bit as quickly.

Information on virtually any or every company and organization is accessible so a consumer, competitor, investor, or the media can bring up any reference—good and bad—that was ever posted or published on a subject. A negative newspaper or magazine article might be forgotten by the next news cycle and comments made on TV and radio are likely to reach only a limited audience giving most stories less than total attention.

But the same system that allows instant global access, the Internet, absorbs and holds every story—or worse, every rumor—and it is "out there" in cyberspace, perhaps forever, waiting for a search engine to bring it to your screen.

In 1999, W. Timothy Coombs, an Associate Professor in Communication at Illinois State University, wrote in the *Journal of Public Relations Research*, "A crisis is a major, unpredictable event that threatens to harm an organization and its stakeholders. Although crisis events are unpredictable, they are not unexpected."

Really? With all due respect to Professor Coombs, crisis events *are* often truly unpredictable, but they are oftentimes also *quite* unexpected.

What makes a problem situation qualify for crisis status is that the person, company or organization at the center of it did not expect it to happen—at least not when it did. Perhaps in hindsight, it is reasonable to suggest they *should have* seen it coming—that they should have read the signs.

Returning to the subject of change, no one seems to doubt the truth of the adage "times change." Disputes, criticism and dislike were once matters settled privately by the parties involved. Today, as part of the effort to put the weight of public opinion behind a position, the media is "worked" very aggressively.

Businesses, both big and small, can devote years—even decades—to building a good reputation, only to have it tarnished by a critic, competitor, member of a special interest group or a news reporter or commentator. Someone making a casual reference to a company or brand being overrated or difficult to work with or "known for" cutting corners and skirting regulations can put the most unsuspecting company on the defensive against rumor or innuendo.

The problem is that a company wishing to defend its reputation can't defend a negative. That is, the company cannot prove it is *not* doing something wrong. There are courts that allow a person or company that has been damaged by such references to seek restitution by way of a public apology and/or a financial settlement commensurate with the degree of damage that can be proved by way of business lost, or appropriate compensation for damage to a reputation. While such a situation attempts to provide fairness and justice, it often is too little too late...

- First, perusing legal action can take years and meanwhile the company or organization at the center of the situation is forced to operate under a cloud with its stakeholders not really being sure if they are dealing with a good, honest or ethical organization.
- Second, if the claims are made in a country other than one's own, laws or regulations don't always follow consistent decisions. What's libelous in one place may not be in another.
- Third, the damaging claims or comments are repeated again and again, sometimes even after much of the public may have forgotten the original incident ever occurred.
- Fourth, the damage is done. Even after a full apology, there will always remain a certain percentage of the public that will question whether the organization is really guilty of the charges and simply managed to get away with wrongdoing.
- Fifth, regardless of the favorable-to-unfavorable balance of coverage or issues of the case, everything is out there in the Internet for an indefinite period of time—perhaps forever.

There is always a risk that some private citizen, researcher, credit investigator, media representative, competitor, or other individual will find only the negative information online and not see any counterbalancing data.

- Six, much of the online content that is available to search engines, because they are used globally to collect information, does not lend itself to translation, so the subject of the material may be victimized by erroneous or unfair references or characterizations.

An imperfect world

In a perfect world, where everyone told the truth and treated others fairly, there would be little need for some types of crisis management strategies or services. Natural disasters would be addressed without putting fault on individuals, companies or agencies for not preparing or responding in a certain way. The problem would simply be addressed and solved; competitors would focus on the quality and value of their own products and services and not engage in "attack marketing" almost wholly aimed at ridiculing, insulting or discrediting other companies or brands; consumers would contract for products and services solely for the legitimate purposes for which they were created and not in the hopes that a problem or flaw will be discovered for which huge amounts of money will be paid to avoid bad publicity.

But it's not a perfect world. Competition is ever more intense and tactics reflect that.

Marketers in the United States never considered saying a competitor's name out loud, much less using the competitors name, package, ad or image in an advertising campaign. In the 21st century such practices are commonplace. Competitors disparage one another in ads, presentations, websites, blogs, live and recorded demonstrations and comparisons, all starting from the simple premise that the marketer—and everyone viewing the ad or presentation— accepts that the announcing marketer's product is superior in everyway to its competition. Thus begins a barrage of smirking, dismissive references to the competitor's inferiority, with a wink at the audience for being smart enough to be on the correct side and make the right and obvious choice. Curiously, such tactics.

From small, dismissive comparisons of inexpensive products—from cola to soap to high-end investments—to references or direct attacks on entire companies and countries—warning the public that every product originating from that country, whether it's toys or tomatoes, should be avoided. Sometimes the warnings may be justified if evidence backs up a claim; other times, in so many instances, the attacks are inconclusive or unfounded, intended to promote fear, uneasiness, uncertainty, or a blatant untruths about quality or safety. Scare tactics work.

"Everybody" says it... so it must be true, right?

Business crises can take many forms. In 2007 print and Internet media carried an important story by Madelaine Drohan, an award-winning author and journalist who has covered business, economics and politics in Canada, Europe and Africa. Ms. Drohan wrote:

> *"Ever since China joined the World Trade Organization in 2001 and began its spectacular transformation into a trade superpower, the chorus of complaints about its low-priced goods has been swelling. China has been blamed for the massive loss of manufacturing jobs in countries such as Canada and the U.S. and it has also been accused of using unfair trade practices to capture an ever-increasing share of the world market."*

If this story would have appeared in only one newspaper it might have been dismissed or "positioned" as an anti-China story by a media company with a particular bias. But its publication was *not* limited to one publication, one website or even one *medium* and the fact that one of the media components involved was the Internet means its text would be available *worldwide* and *forever*. Consider the consequences of that one statement, particularly the last two highlighted words—worldwide and forever. The two words applied to any story at all is significant, but the fact that the words are part of a negative story and apply a negative slant to not just a product or a company—which would have been bad—but two manufacturing, marketing and quality control of seemingly all products from a specific *country*.

What ramifications, if any, might such a story have on a local and global level, relative to pricing, quality, distribution, trade, competition, health and safety, the law, and international relations just for a start?

Internationally, a Difference of Opinion

The cases presented later in this book provide accounts of crisis situations, as well as the solutions, noting how some companies successfully managed their crises. And some that didn't. Cases might be updated, in the sense that they are different named companies, but the principles of how to manage (and market and succeed) in a crisis have remained remarkably the same.

Some things, however, have changed significantly. Technology has altered how people do business and how they communicate—communication being the ultimate necessary device in crisis management.

The other important change is, with the ability of even a small or midsize local or regional business to operate on a global level, international business is not a generic, homogenous proposition. The World Wide Web might have erased borders in many senses of the term, but borders are in fact still there. Regulators in each country may interpret rules and regulation differently and that's something the Internet doesn't stop to explain when it connects someone in Miami, Florida to someone in Shanghai. Just as lawyers differ on their interpretation of laws, conducting business quickly and globally does not mean everyone speaks the same language.

Many crises could have been averted had communication been better.

E-mail is faster than surface mail, which is no minor consideration in an era when everyone wants everything right away, but e-mail is far less personal. It's hard to read someone's body language or tone of voice in an e-mail.

Personal contact is still the most powerful way to advance an idea or manage damage control. It's about being able to look someone in the eye and reinforcing one's integrity and credibility.

In the early 21st century, "eye-contact" is at a minimum. The convenience and "conversational control" provided by electronic communication devices encourage usage between people separated by only a thin wall or space divider. The very products and processes that make communication effortless across the globe, promote minimal face-to-face conversation in the same offices or building. When trying to promote deeper understanding of problem situations and solutions, managing communication is essential, but carrying it to absurd excesses increases the possibilities of miscommunication and misunderstanding, leading to a high-tech state of confusion.

To the greatest degree possible, keep communications simple and direct.

With greater opportunities for businesses locally, regionally and globally, comes the need to understand the exposure and potential new problems that come with them is greater. Opportunities usually have elements of risk commensurate with the potential return: the greater the opportunity, the greater the potential risk.

In 2008 alone, the U.S. and the U.K. were hit hard by problems in the financial industry. Accounts differ on the extent of the damage and who or what is to blame, but no one differs on the fact that extensive damage has been done.

A Financial Crisis of Massive Proportions

Late in the third quarter of 2008 the world watched the richest country in the world approach what its leaders described variously as "a problem", "a crisis" and a "disaster"—and probably the worst such situation in history, possibly exceeding that of the "Great Depression"—the worldwide economic downturn of 1929. Clearly, the resolution of the matter would have global consequences.

The fact that the situation reached a frightening level only one month before the country would elect its new leader, added to the rhetoric and the confusion over the accuracy of the dire predictions. Some suspected the whole scenario—three large entities that were essential to maintaining the country's financial underpinning—were simultaneously imploding.

The story has been widely covered, along with charges and counand countercharges. In reality, there is nothing an average citizen or a single business owner could do to undo the damage and stabilize an economy or reverse business practices. It require government intervention and action to do that.

AIG, one of the world's largest insurers; Merrill Lynch; Wachovia: WaMu (Washington Mutual) are only a few large and famed organizations that folded or were bought, the bottom line registering losses in the range of $350 billion to $750 billion.

China, certainly one of the most powerful countries on earth, experienced crises in its production and exporting of toys, toothpaste, pet food, and even milk products reported to be tainted with a toxic chemical. How do businesses respond—locally or globally—when a country's government has the ultimate final decision of what should or can be done?

Throughout history countries have suffered natural disasters, revolutions, escalated crime problems, and any number of situations that made it off-limits for trade and travel.

The International Monetary Fund (IMF) reported that worldwide losses stemming from the sub-prime mortgage crisis in the United States could run as high as $945 billion.

- People around the world have been brought to a point—more than once—where they are wary and suspicious of businesses' problems, easily inclined to assume "someone screwed up" motivated by greed or something else. It is not enough to be just honest with the public; a response plan must be plausible and must pass "the smell test."

- The response to a crisis must reflect the particular circumstances. That is, do not simply pull out an "off the shelf" crisis management script and try to "Do what Ford did" or "Do what Johnson & Johnson did." The public and the regulators know when they are witnessing a repeat performance of a play they've already seen.

- Speak to specifics. A response plan announced following hurricane damage should not sound like the same response the company tried when it encountered problems on its production line or in its accounting practices.

Whether the crisis is a natural disaster (earthquake, flood, hurricane...) unfair criticism, Internet rumors, misunderstanding, an unfortunate, but true problem situation occurring within a company or organization; bias; children's issues; a disease epidemic, or anything else, rarely or never should crisis management be considered hopeless.

Crises can be serious, but few are irreversible.

Part I

Creating Marketing Relationships

Understanding
"The People Business"

Chapter **1**

Defining a Plan, Building a Business—It All Begins with Trust

Some of the most respected business leaders believe that trust is the cornerstone of a successful business. Some of the most innovative, fast-talking dreamers know that their big ideas will never get off the ground if they can't get people to trust them. A relationship with a banker, backer, or customer has to be built on trust. A marketing effort starts with such relationships and, hopefully, turns into business.

Getting and keeping business has always been a challenge, whether your business is new or old, large or small. Trends, technological advances, population shifts, economic cycles, or just the intensity of competition in a given geographic area are only a few of the reasons why virtually no business in existence can expect simply to hang out its sign and wait for the customers or clients to come pouring in.

In the 1960s, any company with a name that ended in "tronics" seemed to be hot. And then it wasn't. People and business moved on and companies that built reputations and won the trust of consumers had to change with the times or fold. Having something on which to build was often the crucial difference. Sometimes that something was little more than a reputation.

The fast-food industry exploded onto the scene and changed the way millions of people bought and ate their meals. Then the industry peaked, declined, bounced up and down across a few graph lines on the growth chart, and settled into the same type of "we had better be better than just good to survive" mode as other businesses.

People in the securities and financial services industry will admit readily that they could have done without October 1987. And October 1989. Trusting, established relationships were tested.

Two stock market crashes, two years apart and both in October, will certainly find the media approaching future October markets with anxiety, caution, and concern comparable to a departing trans-Atlantic jet. The markets, as airplanes, usually perform as expected, but why not buy that extra insurance coverage just in case.

The financial services industry—managing other people's money—one area where trust and integrity mean the difference between a sale and a long-term customer.

The process of building trust can be especially challenging when customers are particularly sensitive to the market environment.

For example, the author of this book noted a piece published in the *International Herald Tribune* that "despite the popularity of those little yellow smiley-face stickers, it's hard to look a broker in the eye and say 'have a nice day.' Nobody on Wall Street or LaSalle Street has had a nice day for a while now." The article went on at length about "investor uncertainty"—the curse of the investment business. The date of the article was 1974.

At that time, volume on the American Stock Exchange was less than one million shares a day. In Chicago, a new trading operation, The Chicago Board Options Exchange, had recently opened its doors, causing financial experts across the United States to question the sanity of the venture, with interest in the securities market so low and such a high level of investor uncertainty. People were not particularly in a trusting mood.

Students of the markets will remember that, within a year of its creation, the Options Exchange was being hailed as "the hottest game in town… the market that brought a new energy, new life to the sagging securities business." Every other exchange in the country began scrambling to get a piece of the action by developing options programs of their own. Brokerage firms that had waited on the sidelines were racing to set up options departments.

The average age of the trader on the exchange floor was twenty-eight years. Young people who had hoped for a career in the securities industry and found a shrinking investment world suddenly found new doors opening, new career opportunities from which to choose. Seasoned older traders who had fallen on very lean times felt reborn. And all of this was happening at a time when the market climate was terrible and investors were "uncertain." A lot of new relationships were formed in 1974.

Who or what was responsible for this tremendous success? A hundred observers might offer one hundred different answers.

New start-ups in the go-go 1970s weren't only significant in the financial services. The landscape was rich with new ideas and new ventures. Many, however, were said to have one thing in common. Looking back, perhaps one characterization as legitimate as we are likely to get might be attributed to Gordon Gekko, the fictional character of the Oliver Stone film *Wall Street*. Years later, Mr. Gekko would suggest the explanation was simply "greed." Gekko was a takeover artist and inside trader who shamelessly stood up at a shareholders' meeting and intoned into the microphone that the whole point of investing was to make money and that "greed is good." Most people over the years have had trouble publicly embracing such a questionable, politically incorrect trait. Although in the 1980s it was actually fashionable, a simple truth is that investors in any investment will say they want security, stability, and safety.

What they really want is a good return on invested money.

Does a good investment counselor, banker, lawyer, or, for that matter, a marketer, build a relationship with an appeal to a sense of greed or need for security and safety? Or a dream of independence and freedom from financial pressures?

Why did people stop stuffing mattresses and cookie jars with the family savings and start using banks? Society said banks were safer and the mattresses didn't pay interest on the money. Additionally, the banker was a person of integrity. He was trustworthy.

The early 1980s, banks offered a season or two when, as one industry observer noted, the banks all wanted to be brokerage firms and the brokerage firms wanted to be banks. By the late 1980s, banks would have been happy to be *anything* but what they were.

The industry rebounded of course… only to crash again – even harder – in 2008.

When it comes to creating trust, financial advisors, perhaps more than other professionals, are supposed to know their customers' hopes and objectives in order to determine their *suitability* for particular types of investments. Suitability is important enough that a "rule" was named for it in the securities business and the SEC takes it very seriously. Again, it was about trust—about knowing whom you are dealing with and what they want to do.

You can feel reasonably sure investors will not list "lose money" as an investment objective. Investors want to make money and it helps if their investment representatives know this. Sometimes, however, investments, despite the best forecasts to the contrary, move in a downward motion and this leads to investor uncertainty.

In the film *The Graduate,* its main character, Benjamin, was described as a young man uncertain about his future. We might shrug and say that pretty much describes almost everyone at that stage of life. In a sequel of sorts called *The Marriage of a Young Stockbroker,* Benjamin had grown up and become a character named William, who was still uncertain about his future. The message might be that life and the stock market don't offer certainty—in the movies or in the best of relationships.

Uncertainty is a simple reality of business.

The person in business who wants not only to stay in business but to do well must commit to certain truths, the first of which is that people are often uncertain about the wisdom of their decisions.

They look to their lawyers, accountants, brokers, bankers, in-laws, and the companies in which they invest for reassurance.

So reassure them.

Nobody has a magic formula, but there are a few things you can do.

The Personal Approach

To begin with, start taking things personally. Marketing may be a corporate responsibility, but marketing is, no small part, creating relationships and that is everyone's job to some extent.

First, take a look at yourself. While few of us may be able to look at ourselves with any real degree of objectivity, if you want to build trust—to build a relationship with your customer (and hopefully *you* have more than one)—you have to exhibit elements of trustworthiness.

Start with a pen and paper.

Write to people. Our society has programmed us (even the younger generation, as curious as it may seem) to believe something when it is put in writing. Books, newspapers, surveys, reports, memos—if it's in writing it has a stamp of credibility. Whether the person with whom we are communicating is an old and dearly valued customer, client, shareholder, industry observer, or a new prospect, write.

What are you going to write? An enormous number of people, despite their education, often say, almost proudly, "I can't write."

Wrong. That's a weak excuse and there are ways to work around it.

What have you got to say? Here's an example: If you've just spoken by phone, send a short, follow-up courtesy note, offering a sentiment such as "Thanks for taking time ..." One need not be a great writer or a touchy-feely emotional person to share thoughts or feelings effectively.

Whenever possible, say it twice, as in "something's coming," even if it is a piece of your sales literature. Send the literature, or whatever, with a short cover note such as "here's the information I promised to send to you." It might be a revised rate card, a new warranty or discount schedule, or notice of a new offering, a newsletter, or a prospectus. People in virtually every business have *something* that can suit this purpose. Even in an era of e-mail and text messaging, people still respond more positively to receiving an actual written note from someone. If the last thing your business printed was a year ago, make a reference to it and tell briefly how things have changed since then. Note: If they *haven't* changed, perhaps it's time they did; be that as it may, if your printed piece is still current, send it.

Yes, postage rates keep going up, but the purpose here is relationship building, not in saving fifty cents per customer or prospect on correspondence. A phone call afterward asking, "Did you receive the information I sent? What did you think of it? Didn't have time to look at it? Well, sometimes those things can seem a little technical, maybe I can explain it" is courteous, service-oriented, and good business.

In a contact such as this, you have demonstrated:
- Service (very important to most everyone these days)
- Authority (you're going to explain)
- Confidence (sales literature, schedules)
- Credibility (you've put it in writing)

This being the "Age of Technology," isn't e-mail good enough or better than a letter? Go ahead and use it if you choose, but just as the old story held that things could get lost in the mail, things can get lost in space as well. Or, worse yet, your very thoughtful follow-up can go unread in a computer. An actual letter or note that must be opened and handled is as appropriate after you've sent an E-mail as it is after a phone call.

Most everyone in most every business that has seen fit to create a marketing department notes with some conviction "ours is a people business. It's people talking to people. It's how we make our living."

Well, *most* businesses are *people* businesses and people businesses inherently count on trust. This is why effective communication is so important. But, communication also means *listening*. If you listen, you will notice that the word people use most frequently is I.

Listen to what your customers and clients are saying. You want their goodwill (as well as their business), so before you offer your opinion on what's correct for them, ask for and listen to *theirs*.

When you respond to what they have to say, instead of going

directly into your pitch, you will find them much more responsive to your message because you have acknowledged their concerns. This is not rocket science or even basic psychology. It is the kind of simple courtesy that invites courtesy that becomes goodwill that evolves into a good business relationship.

A valuable lesson is in remembering that there are those who listen and those who wait to talk. Your client will know quickly which category you fit into. People like and respect good listeners. They trust good listeners. Your follow-up note can include some very effective phrases like "to follow up on your comment," "I thought about what you said," or "because you seemed so concerned about this, I've put together some information …"

Some people live by the rule of "never put anything in writing." The inference of that is clearly shady. However subtle your pattern of sending notes becomes, it continually reinforces your trustworthiness. It is "relationship building" and that relationship carries an underpinning of trust. Almost any type of business can adapt this approach in some way to fit unique or unusual relationships. In its most simple form, it is not any different from a confirmation of a meeting or appointment or an acknowledgment of a conversation or kindness.

Words, conversations, will be remembered incorrectly or perhaps forgotten altogether. But a note or a letter has a life of its own. This practice becomes even more effective over time. People like to think that as long and as well as you may have known them, you still take the extra time and interest to send a personal note.

Consider too, write when you write. That is, use a pen.

Even with today's shiny, high-speed, word processors and other electronic office equipment, the personal touch stands out. If it is necessary for you to send a standard, typed business letter, below your signature add a "PS" or across the top of your letter scrawl something that will:

1. demand to be noticed and read apart from the formal typed communication
2. reinforce your personal role in the communication

Communicate: Create Your Own Marketing Materials

Whether you are a part of a large, national, or international company or firm, a regional operation, or a one-person office, there are ways you can—and should—distinguish yourself.

If your company or firm has sales literature, reports, brochures, videos, or audiotapes, use them. Send them to your clients and prospects with a handwritten cover note.

If you don't have material, create it for yourself. Send magazines, articles, or clippings with an FYI note attached. People who say "I can't write," especially, have no excuse here. Really terrific writers have done the work for you. All you have to do is share it, pass it on. Indirectly, you end up being credited with bringing the information to your client.

Don't wait for the phone to ring or for a customer to just walk in the door. If you're like most people in business, it won't happen that way. The telephone company's ad campaign offers some great advice: call first. Competitors are calling your customers and clients everyday. Call to say you're putting something in the mail, even if it's just your brochure.

Don't assume that because you haven't had a problem it is not necessary to call between sales or trades or your routinely scheduled conferences.

Don't assume, too, that everything you send gets read. Call. Write it again. The same piece of sales literature sent twice with a note indicating "I don't remember if you were sent a copy of this" reinforces the idea that you care enough to give the matter *your* attention. This is just as appropriate an exchange between a broker or banker and customer, a marketing director and client or branch office manager, or CEO to CEO. It is relationship building, the people part of the business.

Show Confidence and Knowledge

In every conversation, in person or by phone, offer a comment on the business, trends, or a major news story that may be relevant to your situation. Ask your customer's opinion. It may seem like a small thing—and perhaps affected or contrived to you—but people feel better about doing business with people who know what's going on. Of course, they don't expect you to know everything, but they do have a right to expect you to be alert and informed as a prerequisite to doing business with you.

Do Your Homework

The trade press and the business section of daily newspapers carry a great deal of information worth sharing with your clients. Use it to your advantage. Share it. You probably skim several magazines or newspapers each week or month. Let something you learn work for you (perhaps even a review of a business-related book that's not likely to get wide mainstream attention or a newsweekly, trade press, *Forbes, Fortune,* or *Business Week* cover story reference).

Be Responsive

Take phone calls and return them promptly. Or have an assistant or an associate do it. No one—especially a customer or client—likes to be taken for granted. You want them to believe they are important to you. They are.

Many of the most senior people in business give out their home phone numbers or allow their phone numbers to be listed. It may seem like a sacrifice of a part of your private life, but often that can be said of just going into a business or profession. Most people will respect your personal or family time and won't call you at home, but the gesture is worth a lot to you. It underscores the value you place on relationships. If you get a call, it may be the difference between getting, keeping, or losing a piece of business.

You can't control the markets, economy, or revolutions in foreign countries—or in business—but you can control your relationships with existing and prospective customers. Do as much as your resources permit you to do.

For example, write letters not only to your customers and clients, but to newspapers and magazines. Comment on what's going on and exploit your comment. That is, if a magazine or newspaper publishes your letter, photocopy it and send it to your clients or prospects. Your objective is to develop trust and much of that trust will grow out of the quality of service you deliver and your own credibility.

When a publication publishes your opinions, it reinforces in your customer's mind that your opinions are worth something. That credibility should be made known.

The "Do Good" Approach

Building trust begins by being trustworthy. Rebuilding trust, if you need to, involves having a reservoir of goodwill from which you can draw.

Close to home it can be something as simple as sponsoring a Little League team or serving on a local association, committee, or board.

The Marketing Institute, a division of the Institute for International Research in New York, has run seminars on marketing with a social conscience. The idea is to enhance the reputation of your product, company, service, or yourself through "cause-related" marketing—identifying yourself with a worthy cause—or, as the institute puts it, to "do well by doing good." Their advice is far from novel, but encompasses the perfect positioning stance of having gone from the greedy 19805 into the caring 1990s. They note, quite candidly, that "sometimes the simplest ideas are the best ideas. Marketing with a social conscience is a marketer's way of... respecting the environment and, most importantly, respecting your customers... Cause-related marketing enhances the corporate image... Old-fashioned values are back in style."

Make your product or company stand for something: the environment, literacy, the arts, the homeless, animal welfare, children's causes—the list of possibilities is virtually endless.

- Numerous companies participated in the search for missing children with photos and descriptions of the children on milk cartons and other packaging.
- Phone companies offered certain dedicated lines for the use of armed services personnel to call home during the 1991 war in the Middle East.

- The annual Muscular Dystrophy telethon collects millions of dollars from corporate sponsors, helping to find a cure for a crippling disease.
- The Olympics attract corporate participants who compete aggressively for designations such as "the official snack food of the U.S. Olympic team."
- Ronald McDonald House provides lodging for families of hospitalized children. Costs are largely underwritten by the fast-food restaurant chain.
- Earth Day 1990 was one of the largest, single-day, multiple-sponsor, participant, jump-on-the-bandwagon programs in recent history with the potential to increase its momentum each year. If the concept was a good fit for your business then, it might still be.
- AIDS research is a sensitive, controversial social cause attracting more and larger corporate donors each year. Expect to see even more growth here since celebrities in the arts and athletics, particularly, have publicly acknowledged that even the rich and famous are not immune to the disease.

Are there risks to being identified with certain products or companies with causes?

Yes.

Are there benefits?

Absolutely.

How do you weigh the risk/reward factors?

Research, analysis, and discussion.

The primary motivation, of course, must be to be a truly good corporate citizen. You have to really care about doing good or an identification with a worthy cause could backfire with enormous impact. That is, the corporate neighbor fined for dumping toxic waste won't suddenly win friends and influence people by awarding scholarships or sponsoring an Earth Day concert.

The trade publication *Marketing Insights* offered a lengthy examination of "cause marketing" in which it noted a study by sociologist Herbert Blumer who, in the early 1970s, identified a "recurring pattern in the life cycle of causes." Blumer contended that a cause had a "life cycle of involvement" consisting of five stages: emergence, legitimation, mobilization, formalization, and implementation.

Emergence, he said, was when public attention would first begin to focus on the cause, and few people would be influenced by cause marketing efforts. The level of potential controversy would be highest at this time. While identifying with the cause early could offer benefits, there is a major risk of alienating those who oppose the cause.

Legitimation is the stage where the cause becomes more widely known and gains credibility. In terms of influence, the audience is still relatively small at this point and controversy still high. Risk/reward ratio remains about the same as in the emergence stage with cause supporters, those in agreement with the issue, grateful and looking favorably on others who support the cause and opponents adhering to a fully opposite position.

Mobilization is when the general public becomes aware of the cause, but debates ensue over the strategies and tactics for solutions. Controversy lessens as people become more familiar with the arguments for both sides.

Formalization is the point at which a general course of action and a solution emerge and the cause itself becomes more accepted, more "institutionalized." While the cause and its support seem largely mainstream, those who opposed it from the very beginning may still hang on to negative or critical opinions of those who support it.

Implementation sees the plan for addressing the cause put into effect while, as is the case with most issues involving a compromise agreement, some who supported it in the beginning will be disappointed at the final form. To a marketer, the value of open support of the cause at this stage is nebulous, as public support across the board is pretty much assumed. Controversy is minimal at this point, yet some original supporters may view its ultimate evolution with disenchantment. Some support remains, some original supporters may have turned away, but basically the cause has been integrated into the social structure and its marketing value has dissipated.

Some marketers will look at Blumer's perspective and analysis and hold that it contributes significantly as a research evaluation for causes that takes into account the risk/reward potential of cause marketing to the company. They ask: will identifying with this cause at this time help or hurt the company?

Others will view this process as a "fair-weather" approach to championing an issue, believing that if it is not now or in the near future a safe and popular cause, back away. This type of support based on superficial association will likely be of minimal value to the company. It's easy to publicize a corporate contribution to Easter Seals, but not so easy to make known your support of AIDS research. Who will be upset—or for that matter impressed— if the company is one of so many that supports the U.S. Olympic team, but what of support for the United Negro College Fund? Children's birth defects research? No problem. Pro-choice or right-to-life issues? That may be a very big problem.

The public likes to support companies and products it believes in. It tends to not think much one way or another about companies that support only popular, mainstream issues. It doesn't hurt, but neither does it help in ingratiating yourself to your customer.

The company that identifies strongly—and early—with a cause it believes in will likely upset some people, but build a fierce loyalty among that segment of the public that admires strong, independent action, whether it agrees with the subject or not. Admiring terms like *gutsy* and *feisty* come to mind.

Pro or con—should the company publicly support, fund, or champion a cause, or distance itself as much as possible?

Few people get angry over your sponsorship of the Boy Scouts, Girl Scouts, or American Red Cross, but what about:
• American Civil Liberties Union (ACLU)
• Pro-choice
• Right-to-life
• UNICEF
• Greenpeace
• AIDS research/safe sex

- Animal rights
- National Rifle Association
- Handgun control
- Anti-nuclear associations
- Human rights
- Habitat
- Amnesty International
- Common Cause
- Sanctuary
- Operation PUSH
- National Organization for Women (NOW)
- 'Save the Planet
- Save the Whales

Kenneth R. Lightcap, was vice president of corporate communications for Reebok International, Ltd. when he was speaking at a Marketing Institute seminar and said, "when considering the initial philosophical question of whether your company should stand for something, consider your employees, customers, shareholders, and competitors."

A "trendy cause" identification or one unpopular with (and not supported by) a company's own employees could prove worse for the corporate image than no cause identification at all.

The public relations firm of Hill & Knowlton made news taking on the Catholic Church as a client for anti-abortion assignments. Many of the firm's employees were pro-choice and made their feelings public, causing at least embarrassment to both their employer and client. That same issue (anti-abortion) was championed by Domino's Pizza founder Tom Monaghan, while many of his company's employees lined up on the opposing side and more than a few customers said they would not patronize Domino's Pizza for philosophical and political reasons. When the objective is to build a trusted business, one would think a pizza company might not need to burden itself with considerations of a "philosophical and political" nature. Thus, does identifying with a cause become a burden to the company?

Your Good Name

As we are focusing on building trust, consider that how people think of you has no small connection to how you introduce yourself— by name. Some names suggest a sense of security, stability, and substance. Some don't.

Rance Crain, president of Grain Communications and editorial contributor to many of their publications, wrote "People will buy a product at a premium price, because they perceive it to be of high quality, or at a very low price, because they perceive all the products in the category to be the same. ...

"What happened in the 1970s and 1980s is that product after product abandoned carefully staked-out positions as high quality brands flooded the market with coupons and other instant response techniques to grab sales to bolster quarterly earnings. Great old brands... drastically cut back on image-building continuity advertising in favor of short-term promotions ... [and] competitors shot to the lead.

"... ironically, the lack of advertising [left the leader] vulnerable.... It was a vicious circle: the more they cut their prices, the less they stood for in the eyes of their customers, and the less they stood for, the more they were forced to cut their prices."

Brand *image*

Brand *awareness*

Brand *name*

The importance of the brand name in marketing is not a new discovery, it is just too often forgotten.

"The name of a business exerts a powerful influence over the prospects for the products or service offered by the business," Jay Conrad Levinson asserts in his book on "guerrilla marketing." He offers ten rules governing a business name. A few of the better ones are:

- Be sure your business name has absolutely no negative connotations.
- Try to find a name that describes your business, such as Jiffy Auto Lube. Note this name also conveys a benefit.

- Attempt to convey your identity with your name: dignity, largeness, local identification, or quality.

When we hear someone say "I'd stake my name on it," we are supposed to be impressed by the depth of the speaker's commitment to the value of that claim.

The expression "the firm has a good name" really means it has a good reputation or a good image. It means trust.

The marketer who summons the world's most sincere tone of voice and says "trust me," usually doesn't get the nod. Trust is not given for the asking, it is earned—through your good name, reputation, service, and honesty. Little things like a personal note, a phone call, or a magazine clipping earn trust, or big things like a major commitment to an environmental cause, along with, not incidentally, caring and quality service.

And earning trust is very good business.

Further, think in terms of giving your clients bonuses just as we give bonuses to team members, or your executives or managers, for outstanding performance or as an incentive. Offer your customer or client a bonus for Sticking with you in hard times or for loyal patronage. Maybe it is an extension on a warranty, a free service call, free consulting time, airline mileage credits, a day or weekend arranged at a spa or resort (as a joint promotion with dual benefits at reduced, shared cost)—whatever works best for your particular business. The word-of-mouth advertising and public relations benefits of such promotional activities is immense. And that contributes to your constituency believing you are a good person and trusting you.

At a Glance: Building Trust

Person to Person

- Look at yourself. Show personality, consideration. Offer an opinion.
- Communicate. Write notes before and after phone contacts and meetings. Putting it in writing reinforces your trustworthiness.
- Show confidence and knowledge. Ask questions. Provide

answers, even if you have to get them from someone else.
- Do your homework. Pull together material of value and share it.
- Be responsive. Take phone calls and return them. Send follow-up notes and reports.
- Invest in your client. Call early or late, but call. Let your client know how much you appreciate the business.

Company to Consumer
- Do good. Choose and associate your business with a worthy cause or issue.
- Make your product or company stand for something. Quality, integrity, service, good citizenship—any and all.
- Avoid "trendy" causes and issues. Such identifications can appear contrived and superficial.
- Select, publicize, and live by your "good name." Convey benefits. Avoid negative connotations.
- Always remember that smart marketing, good advertising, and astute public relations can help you get business, but service and trust are what help you keep it.

Chapter 2

Building Trust ... Again: Reacting to Crisis

Congratulations!

You've made it. All the hard work, the sacrifice, and late hours have paid off. The enterprise with which you so proudly identify yourself is successful by any standards and whether you made it that way or were offered the opportunity to come on board while the rocket was soaring, you're there. And it feels good. Until . . .

The inevitable. Whatever form it takes—a scandal, a lawsuit, an accident, a vicious article in the press, rumors originating perhaps with a former employee or a competitor, an attack on your entire industry or profession—a shadow is looming large. Suddenly, whatever the cause, the trust of your constituent base—customers, stockholders, the media, government regulators, your employees and fellow workers—is dealt a blow that could be crippling or even devastating. How quickly can you recover? *Can* you recover at all? Is trust—goodwill—once questioned, gone for all time?

Conventional wisdom holds that you can't go home again; that what's gone is gone and that the hardest thing to regain is trust once it is lost.

Well, perhaps not. But it very rarely comes easily. What might have taken years or generations to create and so suddenly seems now to hang in the balance, must be handled with care.

Consider that during World War II it could take days or weeks for accurate accounts of battles or casualties to reach headquarters. People at virtually all levels pretty much just trusted that what they were being told was the truth. By the time the United States saw action in the brief war in the Persian Gulf in the winter of 1991, allied commanders watched the battle scenes on CNN—along with tens of millions of citizens of many countries around the world. What was happening, as it happened, was not just being *covered* by the news media, it was the media putting the audience on the scene in real time.

Forget "spin control"—it was no easy task to convince someone what you wanted them to believe when they had just witnessed the event and reached their own conclusions, independent of interpretation.

In the case of a former mayor of Washington, D.C., videotaped engaging in illegal activities in the summer of 1990, the accounts and testimony became almost irrelevant. The picture, later shown on television, was worth a thousand hours of testimony.

Similarly, a person with a home video camera captured on tape the scene of several Los Angeles police officers beating a down and seemingly helpless suspect. The police department said they would investigate. An angry citizenry shouted, "What's to investigate? We can all see what happened on the tape!"

These incidents, separate and certainly away from the subject of marketing, serve to underscore the immediacy of modern communication as well as its impact. Corporate or personal data is offered instantaneously. For years, a problem, crisis, or even just bad news could be held back from shareholders, regulators, or the general public until at least a reasonable time had elapsed for the story to be represented in a controlled fashion. Not that there still were not investigations or lawsuits, but the panicked reactions were exceptions, not the rule.

Instantaneous communication is only part of the equation.

Another part is the volume of it. There are more people employed in news gathering and coverage than ever before. Despite the constant reports of cutbacks and bureau closings, the numbers are huge and more people enter the field each year than leave it. And "citizen journalists" with camera phones and their own blogs (web logs, a running commentary or journal posted on the World Wide Web) catch the scenes the mainstream media doesn't, often sharing their material.

Cable and satellite television brought a proliferation of channels, many of them news, talk, and business-oriented, all looking for subjects and stories to cover and profiles to run.

Each year, new magazine titles abound.

Once only a relative few press lords, Wall Street tycoons, or corporate magnates were known to the public. Now not only the business practices, but the personal habits and proclivities of an ever-expanding list of boardroom celebrities are grist for the business pages and the TV news shows. The list begins with names like Donald Trump, Rupert Murdoch, Carly Fiorina, T. Boone Pickens, Sam Zell, and the heirs of the late Malcolm Forbes. And the list goes on.

The fortunes of the powerful and the incidental take center stage as the whole world watches: relatively obscure U.S. congressman Newt Gingrich is said to engineer a "revolution" that changes the direction of the American government, catapult's him to the position of Speaker of the House, sees him charged with questionable ethics rule violations and misjudgments that leave him fighting for his political life—and ultimately stepping down—all in less than twenty months and all in public view.

A security guard is hailed as a hero after an apparent terrorist bombing, becomes the prime suspect, claims his life is ruined, gets a tepid pass from the FBI, and threatens to sue the government all in a matter of weeks—before a worldwide audience. Two airline crashes—two airlines; one large and well regarded, the other small and struggling— both threatened with extinction as a worried public demands answers at virtually hourly round-the-clock press briefings.

The oil company executives caught on tape making racist comments and discussing unfair employment practices become the lead story on every network's evening newscast.

The updated list of the latest winners and losers is as accessible as the TV remote control. Film at eleven.

When Your Firm, Client, or Industry Is Hit by Rumor, Scandal, Litigation, or Just Bad Press

Crisis is obviously a relative term. To some, an aggressive competitor moving in nearby constitutes a crisis. To others, it may take a scandal, indictment, or, at the least, an inference of some wrongdoing made public before a crisis situation is seen to exist. If or when bad news hits, whether it be an unpleasant insinuation, rumor, item in the press, or major disaster story, the corporate response correctly is and should be "what is the extent of the damage, short-term and long-term, to both our company and our constituency?"

The company? Obviously.

The constituency? Why?

Because a company that   looks only internally when analyzing a problem will miss seeing a lot. An airline that responds to the news of a crash only in terms of its stock price or its own public image, without showing sensitivity to the victims and their families, will likely find its damage control efforts resulting in as great a disaster as its primary disaster. People who put their lives in a company's hands want to believe the company cares. The oil company thinking of a spill in terms of profits, losses, and stock value, without considering environmental ramifications, is in for a very rough trip.

The public, for its part, wants to know to what extent, if any, the company's problems will become their problems relative to costs, health and safety hazards, and community impact.

The marketplace and the media's first question is always, "What do we know about this company or these people?"

This chapter began by noting the power of the media in determining the impact of a crisis. Consider in the previous chapter the suggestions for building trust. Few of them offer instant results. Writing a positive letter or sending a clipping, note, or some other information to a client, or posting a solid story on a web page will likely get a good reaction, but it is the collective result of doing these things over time that will build your reputation for service, enhance the quality of your relationships, and result in the level of broad-based trust you are striving for. The process can take weeks, months, and, in some cases, years, depending on the point from which you start, the volume of your efforts, and the necessity for depth in the relationship. Consider the people who will say they trust General Motors products based on the performance of only one car; or that they trust the dealer because of the attention and service they received; or that they trust a doctor, lawyer, or broker based on their handling of a single matter.

Sometimes the trust is assumed and established based on the quality of just one referral or endorsement, such as, "See my lawyer and let him take it from there; you can trust him." Or perhaps it's one incident, word-of-mouth report, news media story, or "urban fable" ("I know this Is absolutely true because my brother-in-law knows someone who used to work for the company where it happened") and years of "trust" can go up in smoke. Maybe.

In the same year, one pharmaceutical company had to react to reports that people were being poisoned by one of its products and another pharmaceutical company had to react to allegations that its birth control device was causing suffering and death. The first company not only survived, but is stronger than before. The second company is out of business.

Reacting—responding—to a crisis can be done effectively and ultimately leave a person or company stronger when the crisis is over than it was before the problem occurred. It can also end companies and careers.

Whether the contact is on a personal or corporate level, having an initial base, a relationship, a level of trust, and a "reservoir of goodwill" makes your initial position from which to deal with the problem a lot more solid. It is not mandatory for a successful resolution of the problem or crisis, but it makes the job easier. Any good businessperson does not have to be told twice that anything that can make a job easier is worth considering.

Indeed, there are some who actually believe that a crisis presents the ideal opportunity to distinguish oneself and rise to greatness. Entrepreneur and consultant A. David Silver claims that "a crisis is a growth promoting condition... not only is it possible, but it should also be one's goal to use a difficult period to pole-vault to a higher level of achievement."

Silver suggests that for a company to survive a crisis, the following things should be done:

- Forecast the effects of the crisis.
- Select the right war buddies.
- Create genuine liquidity.
- Buy time.
- Cut costs.
- Learn back-to-the-wall, street-fighter tactics.
- Create a plan to redirect your efforts and company and grow as a result.
- Implement your plan.

The first point speaks directly to the value of creating your initial marketing plan. Forecasting the effects of the crisis, by definition, asks you to look at what's going on in terms of your company, market, shareholders, competition, and resources, and consider all possible scenarios of events and courses that could take you in different directions and the ramifications of each one.

Consider the times this was assumed to have been done, but clearly wasn't. There is no more dramatic example in recent times of an entire industry regarded as the most prudent and conservative, and yet obviously without the necessary safeguards and control mechanisms, as the banking (as well as its stepcousin, the late savings and loan) industry.

They had money, analysts, stringent requirements, and the power to refuse loans, based on ultra-conservative, sure-fire standards.

Society will debate for generations why the wheel fell off this once hugely powerful industry. The number of savings and loan company failures during the 1980s was staggering and the situation is far from stabilized even today. Bad loans, bad investments, and, in some cases, outright fraud, rocked the financial community. The media reported a record number of bankruptcies. Old jokes about grandpa's money being safer stuffed in his mattress weren't so funny anymore.

It is sad, yet important to note now that when disaster hit the S&L industry in 1980, the federal government managed the situation very badly. Who would have predicted that the scenario would be repeated nearly 30 years later, when the government and regulators again took their eyes off the ball and the hugely disastrous crash and record number of bankruptcies would be reenacted.

Consider, too, conditions at some of the most respected investment houses on Wall Street. Members of a once-elite circle of investment banking houses were jolted by losses and driven to the brink of ruin.

In the earlier experience E. F. Hutton, a major national brokerage firm, spent millions of dollars advertising designed to inspire confidence and reinforce its image as a top-line firm. Its investment in expansion, recruiting, and training was similarly huge. Imagine then the stunned reaction of the public when the federal government charged the firm with, of all seemingly petty crimes, kiting checks. This was from a highly prestigious brokerage house. It was as if an environmental group had been charged with dumping toxic waste.

In the eyes of the public, the problems look much larger than they do to even the industry professionals, because prestigious investment bankers such as Lehman Brothers, the subject of *Greed and Glory on Wall Street,* and Salomon Brothers, of *Liar's Poker,* don't allow themselves and their important clients to come to the edge of ruin over the arrogance of a handful of executives.

E. F. Hutton was expected to get its prestigious name in the headlines for practices other than kiting checks.

Investment bankers, once held in the highest esteem, now turn up in the pages of bestsellers with words like *barbarians* in their titles.

Surely, these characters were just exceptions. After all, historically, any profession has been able to get a lot of mileage out of the "one bad apple" analogy.

In 2008 the names of Wall Street giants Lehman Brothers, Goldman Sachs, Bear Stearns, Merrill Lynch and several other prestigious A-list firms again dominated headlines, usually with the word "crash" immediately after.

There surely had to be hundreds or thousands of institutions out there that the public could count on, flags waving and books balanced.

Don't bet on it.

Times have changed and the public, in the face of scary headlines, no longer assumes it couldn't happen to them or their bank, their broker, or even to their government. Public confidence in traditional institutions is at an historic low. Business pages of daily newspapers were once considered by the average reader to be the "kind of boring part of the paper" with stock tables, the Dow-Jones averages, and an investment suggestion or two. More recently business sections are rich with articles and columns on corporate disasters, high crimes, and assorted swindles that often read like a police blotter.

American businesspeople are no longer pictured as dignified, gray-haired patriarch types in pin-striped suits, conservatively managing millions with a quiet, detached, air of confidence.

It's fast track all the way—and the track has an abundant number of dangerous curves.

Cable News Network, the CNBC Financial News Network, MSNBC, FOX News Channel, and investigative television programs, such as *60 Minutes* and *Dateline*, bring the public into the executive suites and boardrooms to see where and how deals are made.

Sometimes a company doesn't even need its own scandal or crisis to have the public's confidence in it shaken.

Guilt by association works very well.

Is the situation all that hopeless? Is the broker, banker, furrier, tobacco company, or oil industry employee—accused, under fire, and hopelessly defensive—left without options?

Hardly.

Crisis management experts agree that the proper response to a crisis starts with three steps:

1. Take the impact of the crisis.
2. Step back and consider the situation calmly.
3. Begin devising solutions.

Experienced consultants in public relations, typically the group charged with devising and executing the strategic crisis management plan, offer this fairly basic advice to clients on managing a corporate crisis: *tell it all and tell it first.*

What both of these bits of advice have in common is that it makes no sense to ignore the crisis. Businesses have learned that a company or industry under fire whose leadership or spokesperson is "unavailable for comment," or "refuses to return phone calls," or "declined to be interviewed or to appear on the broadcast" only tend to compound their troubles by looking guilty even before the jury has been impaneled—by looking as if they have something to be ashamed of.

The grandfather of all mistakes is the phrase "no comment." It goes beyond *implying*—it flatly *states*—that you don't believe people who are to be affected by the issue in question have a right to know what's going on. It thus compounds the problem by forcing the investigators to go to other sources for information, perspectives, or opinions, sources that should not be assumed to be on your side.

Further along, some specific cases will be outlined where things were done both very right and very wrong. But to set up a general framework, a structure within which we can later be specific, let's identify a formula approach to responding to crisis situations:

1. Publicly acknowledge the problem.
2. Investigate (and announce that you are investigating) the range and scope of the problem.
3. Designate a single spokesperson to represent your position.
4. Present and maintain the positioning of the company in a larger context than the problem.

Some public relations or investor relations professionals like to suggest that some segments of your universe hold business or management to a different standard.

Consider which factors inspire trust in a product, service, or company:

- the history of the firm, institution, product, or service
- the reputation of the firm as it evolved during that history, as well as the record of how past problems were handled
- the public's opinion—pro and con—of the founder and/or management
- competition
- word-of-mouth reputation, as compared to media coverage and your own sales literature
- policy regarding customer satisfaction
- convenience of doing business

Consider that trust is based on the customer or client's experience doing business with the company and an understanding of its reputation and products. It is a very tough sell to say in an ad "fifty years of service to satisfied customers" and maintain an overflowing file of unanswered complaints. When a customer calls or writes to a local newspaper or a TV channel's Action Line complaining about both service and lack of service, a company's public claims of "customer satisfaction" look pretty silly.

Ford

Ford Motor Company has a long history of manufacturing quality products and providing service on those products. Its founder, Henry Ford, was respected as an innovator and a legend in American history.

The Ford Foundation was for years a generous and kindly benefactor to many worthy causes that enriched people's lives.

The family and the company had created a reservoir of goodwill from which they could draw if necessary.

And, at various times, it was necessary. The most dramatic example was perhaps when the gas tanks of Ford Pintos, a popular subcompact line of cars, were found to explode into flames upon even the slightest impact. Ford talked about the problem in public, addressed it, made good on customer damage claims, and the company remained a consistently good investment in an intensely competitive industry.

Later, Ford experienced a "rollover" problem with its sport utility vehicles (SUVs). The company blamed the Firestone tires on the vehicles for their apparent inability to remain upright on the road. Firestone claimed the problem was a flaw in Ford's design. The public was getting annoyed. The company eventually stopped its public name-calling with Firestone and reverted to the strategy it used with the Pinto.

Perhaps the biggest reason Ford made it through its various crises over the years is the fact that the company has thousands of vehicles on the roads, in garages and driveways throughout the world. Rather than have their investment in Ford products rendered worthless, the public looked to the company and silently prayed it would give them something -- anything plausible -- to accept as reason for unfortunate crises situations. In a typical situation, however, merely offering "something plausible" isn't enough to dampen a crisis. As with a marketing plan, a clear strategy must be employed to achieve an objective.

While many people like to characterize the world of business as tough, cold, and dispassionate, that is often not the case. People's "hot buttons" are such that they respond to emotional impressions, both positive and negative. A longtime friend/good neighbor/fellow citizen of the community who commits a blunder or is a victim of circumstance doesn't come off as all bad forever after. People are forgiving if they can be convinced the person or company is worthy of forgiveness.

A key point is to not wait until you've got a crisis on your hands before you "get worthy." If you've planted the seeds of goodwill before you need what they will produce, you will likely not only weather your crisis, but will come out of it much stronger.

McDonald's

McDonald's is, of course, the drive-in restaurant turned fast-food giant that virtually redefined *dining out* for tens of millions of individuals and families, especially the younger members of the family.

Primary menu items—beef and potatoes—were certified to be of high quality and prices were competitive or lower.

The company, through its advertising and public relations efforts over the years, has emphasized that the quality of its products, franchises, and training continually set the standard for the industry.

High-profile local and national programs for crippled children and needy families, such as Ronald McDonald House, an inn for families of hospitalized children, won the support and respect of even those who had negative feelings about both fast food and red meat.

McDonald's, at various times, has been accused of numerous types of wrongdoing and noteworthy absurdities, including supporting the Church of Satan and putting worms in its burgers. A woman sued the company, claiming that a cup of coffee she purchased at a McDonald's drive-through window spilled in her lap, causing severe burns. The public reaction to the case was largely—and highly uncharacteristically—sympathetic to the company. McDonald's had amassed such goodwill with its customers and the public at large that people were more inclined to believe the customer was negligent than that the company was.

Ten Steps to Effective Crisis Marketing and Management

Waiting is non-productive and going off in any and all directions, showing signs of panic, won't reassure nervous stockholders or customers. Have a plan.

1. Select a single spokesperson.
2. Don't exceed credibility.
3. Publicly acknowledge the problem before it is acknowledged by someone else.
4. Tell what's being done.
5. Anticipate the worst-case scenario.

6. Advertise your position through press releases and paid ads, and make your spokesperson available. (Note that a willingness to be available on short notice and at odd or Inconvenient times is a plus.)
7. It's fine to have a well-known spokesperson, but don't let your spokesperson upstage your message.
8. Always be well-positioned before the crisis.
9. Accept the counsel of professionals.
10. Put your side of the story in writing.

While some of these points are self-explanatory, others may need some elaboration.

Select a single spokesperson to handle statements and questions on the crisis. An in-house or an outside public relations counsel is usually best equipped to handle this. A good PR person knows what the media needs in order to cover the story completely and fairly; what type of background information will best serve the company's interest in keeping the crisis in perspective; and, to echo a classic phrase, "how to win friends and influence people."

With all due respect, lawyers are usually the worst at doing this and are the ones who most frequently draw the assignment. Lawyers also invented the phrase "no comment" and have never been able to quite grasp how negative an impression it leaves. In fairness, lawyers feel they don't much have to care about impressions, they only have to cover your backside in the legal sense. The fact is it can't be a choice between your public image or just what's legal. You need to be concerned with both.

The greater value of the single spokesperson is to keep executives, employees, and other "sources close to the subject" from contradicting one another and providing fragments of the story that might not always be in the company's best interest, or in the interests of providing the most favorable perspective. Often a CEO will believe it is appropriate to speak directly with media at the first stages of the crisis management. This strategy has both pros and cons: It is good that management wants to be available and open, seemingly forthright with nothing to hide; it is bad in that management is supposed to be the last word on a subject. If

Wanted...
Good Jobs for
Good People

There are big changes underway at AT&T. Exciting changes because we're creating three new companies — each focused on serving customers in a different part of the growing communications and information industries.

But each company faces tough competitors. Each has to work even smarter and leaner. And we no longer need central staffs to coordinate their activities, since each will stand on its own. So we have to eliminate some jobs.

As we restructure AT&T, we're giving the people who will leave us strong financial support and extended health benefits. But our goal is to help find a job for every person who wants one.

Nationwide Job Bank

In addition to helping them find another position within AT&T, we've set up a nationwide job bank for those who can't stay with us.

In less than two months, businesses across America have answered our call for help, sending us over 100,000 job leads within their companies. We're adding unlimited job counseling, as well as relocation, back-to-school and training grants.

We deeply appreciate the customers, suppliers, and members of the community who have supported our efforts to find jobs for the good and talented people affected by the changes sweeping through our industry.

Among The Best Trained Anywhere

These are among the best trained people in the industry, with broad experience in marketing, operations, computer programming, data base management, electrical engineering, accounting, finance, or human resources.

If you have job openings and are looking for skilled people, call 1-800-646-JOBS and let us know what you need. Maybe we can make a match.

R. E. Allen, Chairman

AT&T

AT&T apparently believed it could look like "the company that cares...," but this full-page ad in the national edition of the *New York Times*, asking for jobs for employees it was cutting from the payroll, seemed both overtly self-serving and hypocritical.

Outplacement is a fine service, but there are limits to how good it can make a company look. The employees would probably rather have had the money.

the investigation is only begun, a CEO should not reasonably be expected to have enough information to make a strong, reassuring, or factual case.

As CEO, he or she will be *expected* to have all the information. A spokesperson can promise to look into a matter and be forthcoming with a statement, but will not be expected to know everything. When A. David Silver uses the expression "buy time," this is one way to do it. The spokesperson becomes not only the conduit for information, but the gatekeeper, the palace guard. There's nothing sneaky about this, deliberate as it is. You need as much time as possible to prepare your response. This is one way to get it.

While the single spokesperson should coordinate and handle the flow of information, that information should be substantive and plentiful. That is to say, position statements and backgrounders for the media; position statements, newsletters, memos, and backgrounders for the entire internal staff, asking them not to discuss publicly the crisis situation with members of the media, but to direct all inquiries to the designated spokesperson. Keep the staff informed. Don't let uncertainty build from within. Stabilizing the situation within the company is a major step in presenting a strong front to the outside world. Keep your own people informed, but ask that they not offer opinions outside of the corporate family.

To say "Don't exceed credibility" seems like simple common sense, but people do it all the time. Not being totally honest can keep you always on edge with a justifiable fear of discovery compounding the problem.

Bad

In situations such as that of Audi Motor cars, where an alleged malfunction caused the car to accelerate without the driver being in control, the company's first "official" on-the-record responses seemed to attribute the problem to driver error—several *hundred* drivers, committing the same error, using the same model vehicle in only that same model year. To no one's surprise, the public was not convinced. As the expression goes, "It didn't pass the smell test."

Worse

The Exxon seagoing tanker *Valdez* involvement in an oil spill off and along the Alaskan coastline was explained in a way that strained the company's credibility beyond even the point its own employees could accept.

To publicly and honestly acknowledge the problem before someone else does is the first best step to damage control. If you admit there is a problem, explain that you're investigating, and that a more complete statement, analysis, or report is forthcoming, you have satisfied appropriate initial legal and public information demands. A statement, rather than a response to an inquiry, allows you some control over early news coverage. A spokesperson who says too much or tries to fix responsibility too early, or whose story appears too neatly "packaged," becomes immediately suspect. Reporters will probe ceaselessly. Do not get drawn in by engaging in exchanges that can only hurt, embarrass, or complicate your damage control efforts.

To acknowledge what's being done can be as simple as saying: you are cooperating with authorities, investigating, or considering your options, or all of the above. Remember that the media is looking for a comment from you, as, perhaps, are your shareholders, employees, and regulators. Give them something they can use so they can continue to support the organization with a sense of confidence.

Anticipate the worst-case scenario. At minimum, allow for the possibility that the worst could happen and plan for that contingency.

Some discussions of crisis management suggest it might be helpful "role-play" interviews, tough questions, and embarrassing situations. Role-playing is fine if you've always dreamed of being an actor or a psychiatrist, but asking a simple question about how bad things can actually get and what can be done to avert such things is probably sufficient. Above all, crisis situations are the times to save the theatrics and stick to common sense.

Advertise your position through press releases, paid ads, and the availability of a speaker, but don't stop there. In our discussion on building trust, recommendations included writing notes and letters, calling your constituents on the phone, and sending articles, surveys, and studies. In rebuilding trust, this process is even more useful. While lawyers usually don't like this approach, the public generally does. Lawyers, admittedly with some justification, believe that "containing" a crisis makes it easier to get through. Containing, however, is not the same as going underground and hoping or waiting for things to blow over. Control your crisis by taking the lead. If yours is the company or industry under fire and you limit your public statements only to responses to reporters' questions, you create an impression of being defensive (which you are being) and that you are appearing to be hiding something, encouraging your critics to push even further.

You also let your critics determine the focus of the story and run the risk that you end up with a story weighted heavily with negatives. Some of the most successful examples of crisis management involve "going public" and taking the initiative, getting the company's side of the story out early, sometimes even before a plan has been fully developed. Coming out first with an "open letter to our customers" or an "advertorial" suggests leadership, forthrightness, and integrity.

"Oh, no!" the legal department screams. "We could be looking at millions of dollars in lawsuits! Why say anything?"

Because it is important to still have a company left when the crisis has passed. If the issue is one of health, safety, or damages, the lawsuits and settlement of damages will likely be there whether or not the company positions itself on the high road as opposed to responding and ducking or avoiding response altogether.

An open letter, a quickly produced television message, letters to shareholders, regulators, and the general public, built along the lines of "... our company is currently the subject of much attention and concern. We want you to know that we are doing everything possible to seek a speedy resolution to the situation. We have a history and a reputation of service and that service does not end now. We thank you for your patience, your understanding, and your support."

This type of response is vague and unspecific enough to prevent the lawyers from screaming (though they will) and open enough to help shareholders and the public continue to believe in the company while you proceed with the necessary next steps.

Consider this case study:

The Jewel Food Store chain saw its name and logo on the evening news as accounts of people with salmonella poisoning were reported. The media suggested that the common thread in every case was that the victims had consumed milk purchased at a Jewel store—and that it was milk from the company's own dairy. After numerous cases were reported, Jewel responded by closing the store thought to be the distribution point of the suspected contaminated product; sanitizing the entire store before reopening days later; closing the dairy that was the alleged source; working closely with health inspectors; substituting a brand of milk other than its own house brand on store shelves; and running full-page newspaper ads, in-store signage, and high-exposure television spots in which the company's CEO urged consumers to pour Jewel milk down the drain and bring the empty container to the nearest score for a refund.

While what remaining product still in homes was probably not contaminated, Jewel said it didn't want to take any chances with its customers' health while it set about learning what had happened. A full investigation was underway and the company would spare no effort to make things right.

The company-owned dairy never reopened.

Lawsuits by alleged victims and families were filed and settled quickly.

Jewel Foods had heavily advertised itself for more than two generations as a "neighborhood store" (despite its being the largest chain of stores in the area).

It had consistently stressed customer service in its ads, guarantees, and sales.

It is still today the most successful chain of food stores in its market.

When Products and Superstars Are Not a Good Fit

Product spokespeople are supposed to get attention—especially among their fans—and their appeal is supposed to reflect on the brand, product or company paying spokesperson's fee. But sometimes the celebrity spokesperson can upstage the product and its message. This is a problem, it seems, for even the largest companies.

The investment firm of E. F. Hutton hired comedian Bill Cosby as its spokesperson following their check-kiting scandal. Mr. Cosby, at the time one of the most recognizable and popular figures In the United States, had no known direct connection to the firm and, one might have assumed, being a man of enormous wealth, left his own investment decisions in the hands of lawyers, accountants, and business managers. The strategy of using Mr. Cosby in print and television advertising to say how much he trusted the firm proved to be a very expensive bad idea. While the ads received considerable attention, audiences wanted to know, "What's he doing here?"

Other large companies have hired such high-profile individuals as former Secretary of State Henry Kissinger as "consultants." What they were actually buying was the identification with a prominent person's reputation. True, some people want high-profile political figures on their boards or on their payroll to provide advice, counsel, and access to other high-profile political figures. Others want only an association with the individual's reputation. Especially in times of crisis, a company's "out-front person" or "face" should be someone who is identified with the company—its CEO, Chief Operating Officer, or PR specialist. To bring in a well-known, but obviously uninvolved with the brand, person will merely suggest that the company "bought" a particular spokesperson to increase or raise concern about Its willingness to be candid.

Here's a better idea: Be well-positioned before a crisis occurs.

The late billionaire Howard Hughes (and a few other prominent public figures) reportedly had paid PR people to keep their names out of the press.

A number of actors and business executives boast that they always refuse requests for interviews. Another bad idea. These are often the same individuals are shocked and wounded when, as they find a problem engulfing them, the media and the public appear unsympathetic to their plight.

A CEO, after having refused to be interviewed for a story in a national business magazine, was angry upon reading the story, bellowing at his company's PR man "Can't you control your press buddies? He's got me looking arrogant and egotistical' How's that going to look to our stockholders?"

It would likely look exactly as it looked to the reporter. No one is suggesting that a company or its management should be guided for appearances only. PR people can't and don't control "their press buddies." They can usually influence the tone of a story by providing access, cooperation, honesty and useful information. A company's point of view is normally (though, not always) represented fairly and accurately when the company's people take and return phone calls and provide requested information.

Consider this: If a shareholder calls or writes for information on past financial performance or corporate philosophy on long-range goals, odds are the information would be provided immediately. That's the nature of company/shareholder relations. But if the same information were requested by a reporter, many corporate offices would kick into a defensive, evasive mode. Wrong strategy. The company whose people ask the reporter how they can be of assistance, making clear up-front their legitimate interest is in getting the company's story told accurately, finds the media usually willing to be more than fair—even favorably disposed toward the company in difficult times.

Accept the counsel of professionals. Remember the saying "Those who can, do; those who can't, teach"? Well, many people feel that way about consultants. The question is often asked: Why should you call someone who is not in your business to advise you on what is best for your business? That assumes you would ask them to be involved in the same things in which you are involved. Consider that a doctor doesn't call another doctor to help him with his tax audit.

Advertising and public relations people—marketers—often

believe they can handle their own troubles when dealing with the media or the public. After all, that's their job. They do it all the time.

In crisis times, however, there is a need for objectivity and the ability to identify the "worst-case scenario" that insiders often lack. A competent advisor in times of trouble is like research. Even if all you learn are things you already know, it was worth the investment to make certain you were correct.

What if the opposite had proven true? The synergy of the insider and outsider perspectives is important in satisfying yourself and your constituents that you have made the maximum effort to contain and control a crisis and your response to it.

Having agreed to call in the reserves, accept their counsel. A client who hires a professional to agree with him or her is wasting everyone's time and money, and exhibiting the kind of attitude that may well have contributed to the crisis in the first place.

Putting your side of the story in writing is a reiteration of a recommendation in our earlier exercises in building trust. People tend to believe not only the written word, but the writer. If you have shown the willingness to write an open letter or an advertorial, you have both enhanced the chances of your message being reported and repeated accurately, and made a statement about your candor and openness, "positioning" which in itself can be used to your advantage.

At a Glance: Building Trust Again— Reacting to Crisis

To review the strategies for maintaining and rebuilding trust:
- Prepare a situation analysis. Determine what might need to be added or changed relative to your original marketing plan.
- Select a single spokesperson, someone who understands the art and science of effective communication, to provide information and answer questions for your side.

- Don't exceed credibility. Be honest.
- Go public with your problem before someone else does. Be honest.
- Acknowledge what you're doing about it. Ramifications of a crisis are increased when the subject compounds the problem by lying or trying to minimize its importance.
- Anticipate the worst-case scenario and plan for it, if only as a contingency. The motto "be prepared" is no less a good strategy for the marketer than it was for the Boy Scouts.
- Advertise your position through letters, paid ads, press releases, newsletters, and the availability of a speaker.
- Control your crisis by taking a leadership position in public. Be first with the statement; don't wait to be asked or let your critics shape the story.
- Don't let your spokesperson upstage your message. Attempting to buy an outsider's credibility is a risky and misguided strategy.
- Create and draw from a reservoir of goodwill. Be well positioned before the crisis.
- Accept the counsel of professionals. Look for objectivity to be certain you haven't overlooked any possible strategies.
- Be willing to put your message in writing as a way of reinforcing your integrity. And be honest.

Chapter **3**

Timing is Everything ... or Is It?
Doing Business During a Crisis

There's always a reason for uncertainty. Nevertheless, there truly are periods when even the most positive mental attitude in the brightest marketer and the top producer may run into a problem making the sales connection.

Scenario: You are a thriving community savings and loan with a great location, good reserves, an efficient staff, and a well-lighted, newly paved customer parking lot. Or, you are the most visible, widely advertised, and prosperous tile and carpet center in your community. Or you're a thriving distributor of imported motorcycles.

No matter.

The front-page story in the morning paper told the world in general—and your customers in particular—that your industry is in trouble. Incidentally, your management and your bank have just authorized the purchase of property across the street for expansion. They are expecting you not just to hold, but to *increase* your customer volume.

Some might call this the worst possible time to have to generate new business.

Scenario: You are a broker with thirteen years experience and make a good living. You are honest, capable, and your employer is one of the top brokerage firms in the nation. When they talk, people listen. As you anticipate a day of either very light or very heavy market activity and consider which of any number of attractive recommendations to share with your customers, the morning news tells you—and your customers—that the federal government has charged your firm and its management with a number of federal and SEC regulatory violations. As your heart races at the absurdity of such allegations, you hear that your firm has conceded the violations and, in a settlement, has agreed to pay millions of dollars in fines and accept certain other humiliating sanctions in order to avoid a process that suggests things might get worse.

You slump in your chair. You think this must be just about the worst possible time to be in your position. Yet, you *are* in your position and you have to go to your office and explain to all those people, to whom you have boasted (not unreasonably) about your firm's integrity, that you've got, er, a problem here.

Some expressions seem destined to survive the ages, if not *define* the ages. Just as the phrase "investor uncertainty" can actually be applied to virtually any market at practically any time, another phrase that won't go away is the one that holds that a particular condition represents the "worst possible time" to do business.

Of course, to some people this has been an excuse for failed careers and failed businesses since time began. Just as the top producer seems to always be the top producer (often to the amazement of colleagues), to many individuals, whether the economy is up or down, the season is right or wrong, or new tax laws are about to signal change—it will always he the worst possible time.

The car dealer who sells a popular model with a gas tank that explodes on impact, the other car dealer with the model that sped up by itself, the furrier, and the tobacco company marketer—all have to believe this is the worst possible time to have to go to work.

Here again is an instance where the term crisis becomes relative.

Is a scandal or bad press a business crisis? Yes.

Economic recession seems to be an almost cyclical occurrence. It must be assumed that because times are good in a given period, they won't always be good. Isn't a crisis a time in which your customers stop calling or can't pay their bills? Of course.

Aggie Jordan, CEO of Jordan-DeLaurenti in Dallas, Texas, tells her clients, "There is no recession. If you admit there is one, you'll be in a negative mode and won't be out there selling because you'll believe there isn't any business."

Ms. Jordan herself refuses to acknowledge bad market cycles. Her business has thrived during periods many called the "worst possible time." To many people it would seem silly to deny bad market conditions. Yet, Ms. Jordan can point to her success as legitimate testimony to the power of her approach.

Sometimes a situation is so clouded with adverse influences that the whole idea of trying to do any business seems absurd. Most everyone in business has had hard times like these—when the obstacles seem so great you find yourself using expressions like "It would take a miracle."

There is a sign on a building in Chicago. The sign reads "Expect a miracle."

The building is a church.

Some might say that, in a really lousy market climate, it would have to be.

Think, for a moment, about the habitually upbeat people in your business who go through life expecting miracles and the ones expecting rain.

The optimist and the pessimist—the glass is half empty or half full—the story of two kids, one who always expects the worst and another who, while shoveling out a roomful of manure, says, "With all this horse___, there must be a pony!"

So, should the response to lousy markets simply be a positive mental attitude? Can just refusing to accept adversity make everything turn out all right? Is life a cabaret, old chum?

Hardly.

Attitude, however, is no small consideration in successful

marketing efforts.

Norman Vincent Peale, for example, didn't actually have to think positively himself. All he needed to do was write books in which he advised *other* people of "the power of positive thinking" and he became very, very wealthy. Dr. Peale, however, did think positively and insisted he could control his life with attitude, not the other way around.

The Chicago Board Options Exchange opened its doors for the first time in April 1973, when the stock market was experiencing a period of booming indifference from investors. Aside from receiving such discouraging words as "What do those grain traders in Chicago know about starting a securities exchange," kinder, gentler people dismissed the effort simply as the worst possible time to start a new exchange.

Of course, there would not be a story worth telling if the Chicago Board Options Exchange had not gone on to become not only an instant success, but the success story of the decade.

Those who bought seats on the exchange in 1973 for $10,000 saw the open-market price of those same seats rise to a quarter-million dollars within just a very few years.

Thousands of careers were launched and other U.S. exchanges quickly scrambled to copy the process and get into the business—all at the worst possible time to even consider such a venture.

Something that probably won't surprise marketing professionals who have "been through the wars" is that the things that must be done to develop a good relationship with customers or clients are not dramatically different from the things you do to rebuild.

Many of the same techniques take on a more dramatic impact in a bad market environment, but the basic fundamentals, the principles of good marketing, don't change because the market climate changes. We use a different drill bit to make a hole in concrete than we use for wood, but we still use a drill.

Every case is different, every company is different, every plan is different, but the formula—the framework—is pretty much the same. It's also very important that the formula be implemented at both the corporate level and the personal level.

Richard Poe, senior editor of *Success* magazine, likes to describe himself as a *cultural adventurer*, exploring profit opportunities in the wilds of American society. He writes that "in the 1990s, a whole generation is rediscovering the secrets of a positive mental attitude."

Joe Nuckols is the founder of Winner's News Network, a 24-hour motivational radio station in Ft. Lauderdale, Florida. His station began showing a profit only ninety days after its 1987 start-up and went on to become syndicated nationally. "The 1990s is the decade of positive thinking," said Mr. Nuckols.

From the greedy 1980s to the positive 1990s to the turbulent 2000s, the jury is still out on how much a positive attitude can help, but it sure can't hurt. Pretty much everyone agrees, however, that one of the worst things we have to deal with in down markets is our own attitudes.

At a time when recession headlines were creeping across front pages from coast to coast, seemingly from out of nowhere, video stores appeared—not like department stores or supermarkets—like mailboxes. They were everywhere.

With a new generation of southeast Asian immigrants, came Thai and Vietnamese restaurants—also seemingly everywhere.

Video stores? Restaurants? Didn't anyone tell these people this was the worst possible time to start a new business?

Apparently not. They did it.

And the video stores were crowded throughout the 1980s and 1990s. VCRs and DVD players are in every household, where they were once only an expensive toy of the very wealthy.

And fax machines. And cell phones. And the Internet. "Where did these things come from?" the slightly amused public wonders. While many businesses were not too long ago looking for more efficient ways of licking stamps, virtually every business now wonders how it ever got along without e-mail.

Still, the 1990s was described as a time of soft markets. People didn't have disposable dollars. Uncertainty had become a fact of life. Budgets got tighter by the second.

Still, in Chicago some 600,000 people subscribed to cable television during a two-year period, spending more for basic TV service, plus a couple of extra stations, than they did for their telephone service—which, by the way, they thought was too high—at a time when the city was still not fully wired for cable.

When times are tough and money is tight, but people are going to live their lives anyway—so marketers might as well just accept it.

People are going to buy houses, cars, clothing, iPods, take vacations, and make investments.

It is not the marketer's choice whether or not people will buy; it is the buyer's choice and it is the marketer's role to offer that buyer choices, service, and incentives and to sell at all times as if a significant number of people wanted to buy.

They do.

Joe Cappo, publishing director of the trade magazine *Advertising Age,* pointed out in *FutureScope: Success Strategies for the* 1990s *and Beyond,* "One important advantage that will help most Americans cope with the problems of the next decade is their growing financial sophistication. The vast majority of the people in this country have a better notion of personal finance than any other previous generation. . . . And they learned the hard way. As a result of all this practical education—added to their academic education—Americans today have become conversant with such macro-economic topics as the national debt, the price of gold, the foreign trade deficit, and the relative values of world currencies."

Although Mr. Cappo's words were prophetic, the growth and education never actually peaked, and, in the increasingly higher high-tech era, Americans have a hunger for information greater than ever before. Cable News Network, MSNBC (the joining of the technology and capabilities of Microsoft and NBC television), CNBC, *Fortune, Forbes, Business Week,* and a broad spectrum of other media, once only of interest to a select segment of the population, are watched and read regularly by millions of consumers.

Life insurance salesmen like to say, "Show me a man with a million dollars in life insurance, and I'll bet I can sell him another million because he's a believer."

In both good times and bad, your best prospects come from among your current customers.

The Personal Touch: Going Person to Person

When times are good, pay close attention to your customers. Write, phone, e-mail, and send newsletters and articles. Remind them how much you appreciate their business.

When business is down, double your efforts in this area. Your customers and clients are someone else's prospects. Don't forget that and don't forget your customers. Whatever your business—retail or service, national or door-to-door—young, small accounts and large, well-established accounts have this in common: they both hate to be taken for granted.

Remember that while you keep telling yourself how hard it is to make a buck, that this is the worst possible time, the paper that day will have at least a few stories about new products, new pieces of business being awarded, and new offices, stores, and buildings planned for opening. Let other people's optimism reflect on you.

It will not shock seasoned marketers to learn that the loser is the one who sits in the office, waiting for business to roll in and talking about how times are tough.

Go after new business at the worst possible time.

How?

This will be very profound: the way you do it is to do it.

It's not just an amusing coincidence that many of the top people in business do not all radiate excitement or personal charisma. The one thing so many seemingly bland, gray-suited, white-shirt types have in common is a simple determination to succeed, not to accept that "people just aren't buying" when it is obvious that somebody is making money.

Why shouldn't it be you?

A large national retail chain's CEO was under fire. Associates said that, while he was brilliant in so many respects, he couldn't seem to grasp the idea that there were business cycles. He was continually revising his "strategy" to where the days were all about meetings, not about *doing*.

One need not be brilliant to understand that strategies are good, meetings are fine, but the time comes when there is no substitute for *doing*.

Meeting adjourned. If yours is the type of personal contact business where this can be effective, pick up the phone and call current and past customers or clients. Discuss what the current market climate means to them in the most appropriate way to relate it to your business and be open to the possibility of doing some business. If no business materializes through this call, it has become a public relations/customer service call, the benefit of which is goodwill and the prospect of future business.

Who are we talking about here?

The banker? The broker? The insurance agent? The book publisher or manufacturer's rep or the marketing vice presidents overseeing them?

Yes.

The companies are different, the products are different, but the need for contact is the same.

Clip items from the newspaper and business press and send them to the clients and prospects on your list with your short, personal comment note attached.

Phone to tell them you've just put something in the mail to them and follow-up with a call later to ask if they received it, and to remind them it came from you.

Ask about their current situation, how the "tough times" may be affecting them, what you might be able to do to help.

Any changes in their needs and objectives?

Listen for opportunities, but don't try to rush a close or a sale.

Send information that speaks to their needs. It's out there and easily accessible online and in print in magazines, newsletters, and daily newspapers. And give examples of your own experience and knowledge.

And follow up.

If you move too quickly, you might be dismissed as a salesperson pushing something your client might not yet be ready to buy.

If you listen and respond, you are reacting to their needs.

A nice touch is to share information and observations among your clients. Tell something interesting you've heard from one client to another client, especially something positive about the economic or investment climate and especially in a down market.

To some people this may seem a rather simplistic approach to marketing in bad times. It does, however, work.

A suggestion from Don Beveridge, of Beveridge Business Systems, is on target in any market; "Sell your client a solution to a problem, not just a product. Analyze the end user's need for a product first."

Increasingly, the method of choice is to stop selling and start helping. Your client, customer, or prospect will be a lot more receptive to your efforts if you are perceived as doing something for him, instead of to him.

Some advice from sales training expert Alan Cimberg:

- Be a sharp listener, not a fast talker. A sale moves forward when the prospect does most of the selling.
- "No" doesn't mean never. It means "not at the moment." Try again later.
- Sell the decision maker. When you are selling hand organs, don't talk to the monkey.
- Tell the truth. You won't keep the business if the product doesn't live up to its billing.
- "Your price is too high" means that its value has not been justified to the buyer.

Consider collecting some comments, quotes, or questions into a newsletter that you might e-mail to customers and prospects. Or print one up and mail it. People tend to like to see their names in print, to feel like something they have said is important and quotable. A newsletter you've mailed with their names in it might not be the same as seeing their names in the *New York Times,* but it is still a compliment to them.

Virtually every contact represents a business opportunity. If yours is a company whose marketing efforts are supported by sales literature, brochures, video, and online resources, use them. If you don't have such materials or a budget that allows you to buy them, create your own from business publications and newspapers. Identify the source of the material. It is not only the courteous and legal thing to do, but it both enhances the credibility of the material and identifies you as someone who stays on top of what's being written or said.

Many large companies do not encourage middle management and sales representatives going off on their own to become great publishing moguls of newsletters and other marketing materials. It's not within their corporate culture. Lawyers howl. Usually, however, they have things you can use so you don't have to create your own. Use this material.

Remember, the snappiest, most powerful and colorful sales literature, surveys, and market analyses are completely worthless until you get them into your clients' hands.

As the phone company put it so beautifully, reach out.

Make the contact.

Make the call.

Send the letter.

Yes, there are things being done, hopefully, at the corporate level that will create an umbrella for your person-to-person efforts, but despite what some of the costly "proven" training programs preach, having your sales and marketing people call (even pre-recorded calls) prospects during dinner or on weekend mornings is rarely a good idea. You may indeed find more people at home—and very annoyed at the intrusion as well.

Whether making a cold call or following up on a referral, a polite approach is to precede the call with a note that says you will be calling. A piece of paper, an envelope, and a stamp are your investment in enhancing the quality of your call.

If your firm requires that the marketing and sales force make cold calls—*now*—then it's a good idea to indulge your employer. But remember, and advise your associates to remember, that none of you are morning drive-time disc jockeys, weather forecasters, or stand-up comics. Be pleasant and businesslike, use your own voice, and get right to the point (make the "Hi! How are you today?" greetings the least intrusive and annoying as possible).

Ask for permission to send literature for a prospect's review. Whether your company is trying to interest someone in a printing press, a syndicated television show, vitamins, or an investment account, you've probably got some literature you can use. Use it.

People like to hold, review, and file things. It's that "I got it in writing" sense of legitimacy issue again.

If your prospect agrees to look at whatever you are sending, you have just elevated him or her from a cold call to a really qualified prospect.

Particularly in down periods, it is wise to break up cold call cycles with a service-oriented call to a client you believe is content. If it proves this client is not content, your call was not a waste of time. If the client is truly content, he or she will likely appreciate the fact that you called just to check in. Responding to complaints and concerns has actually been shown to *improve* relationships. This is a nice break from cold calling and the rejections that are part of the process and it truly has its rewards.

Consider again your attitude and your mind set. In negative market climates, your negative attitude will only compound the problem and make achieving your success—and even just the performance of your duties—that much more difficult.

"In hard times, some people still become incredibly successful," says New York-based Nancy Raimonds, founder of Unlimited Resources Centers, whose business offers training programs.

Hard times, like a crisis, are relative. Few would challenge that a savings and loan or banking marketer was facing a crisis marketing situation in the 1980s and 1990s. To other business enterprises, from small businesses to huge industries such as the airline and hospitality fields, a recession and its accompanying "cutbacks" and "slowdowns" clearly represented a crisis condition.

Of course, the fact that economists and the government argue tirelessly as to what exactly qualifies to be called a *period of recession* is beside the point. Amazingly, those responsible for running businesses don't have to wait for the technical or scientific designations. They have this uncanny ability to recognize that business is bad when business is had.

Orders drop off.

People stop coming in.

Sales decline.

Jerry R. Wilson, in his book *Word-of-Mouth Marketing,* asserts that you can't eliminate negative talk, but you can minimize it by giving angry customers outlets such as hotlines or customer surveys so they can share their complaints with you instead of with your prospective customers.

In a tape called *Success Secrets of Self-Made Millionaires,* Brian Tracy offers twenty-one principles that are intended to motivate, inspire, and pretty much generally leave you pumped-up about your challenging tasks. Six of them are:

- Never think about failure.
- Set clear goals.
- Associate yourself with successes and successful people (avoiding the negativity of associating with habitual underachievers).
- Be honest with yourself and others.
- Be utterly persistent.
- Discipline yourself.

We've skipped such points on Mr. Tracy's list as "dream big dreams." While that may very well be a quality or characteristic common to self-made millionaires, the point of this work is to respond to tough times and the challenges of bad market conditions. If you accidentally become a millionaire or your company ends up on the *Fortune* 500 list, congratulations. Not everyone is a visionary, nor does he or she need to be. Many marketers are very entrepreneurial in style and nature, always looking for the "new and different" edge; many are technicians who rely on formula approaches to effective marketing. The right approach is the one that works for you.

In an excellent book called *Getting It Right—The Second Time,* former public relations executive Michael Gershman offers his version of marketing in bad times, under bad circumstances, or when simply misjudging the market. He summarizes nearly fifty examples of companies and products that became phenomenally successful after first failing. Some you may have heard of, such as Life Savers, Dixie Cups, Wheaties, and Kleenex, to name just a few.

Mr. Gershman stresses twelve "p" words to make the sale and introduces each with an admonishment:

1. Don't pitch the wrong way.
2. Don't rule out a ride via piggyback.
3. Don't underestimate public perception.
4. Don't incorrectly position your product.
5. Don't overlook the package.
6. Don't sell it in the wrong place.
7. Don't price it wrong.
8. Don't fail to consider using a premium.
9. Don't skimp on promotion.
10. Don't underestimate the power of publicity.
11. Don't launch a product without a promise.
12. Don't quit. Have perseverance.

Some might take Mr. Gershman to task for his choice of leading with the negative. Listing the words in the form of a checklist would basically offer the same good advice. Whether as a checklist or as a list of warnings, consider these twelve points worth reviewing before finalizing your marketing program. In fair weather, they are useful in helping you to stay on track; in a storm—a crisis—any and every assist is welcome.

Hundreds of books have been written on variations of the "positive thinking" theme. Many have become more than bestsellers, they're perennials. Such titles as *Think and Grow Rich, Psycho-Cybernetics,* and, of course, *The Power of Positive Thinking* have never been out of print over the decades. They are bought mostly by individuals (brokers, insurance agents, sales representatives) who have been drawn to their respective professions by the lure of potentially very good income without heavy lifting. The problem is, once on board, they seem to need constant reassurance. The books, the tapes, and the motivational lectures and seminars are as much a part of the routine as the rate card. This suggests one of two elements may be missing: 1) enough knowledge of the business to be confident of its inherent value; or 2) belief in the value of the product.

To use a phrase consistent with the positive thinking approach, if you think your product is tough to sell, you will be proven correct.

One of the toughest parts of being a life insurance salesperson is believing that either people don't need your product or that they *think* they don't need your product, making selling them a monumental task. The people in the insurance business who treat it virtually as a religion, believing their product is as basic a necessity as electricity and a car, sell millions of dollars worth of insurance every year. True, they are, in many cases, annoying in their persistence, enthusiasm, and their "answer for every conceivable customer objection," but they do sell a lot of insurance.

At the risk of over-simplifying, if you really believe this is the worst possible time to be marketing your product, then it truly will be. If, however, you believe that since your product has value and that there is a need for it, a use for it, and a market for it, *sell* to that market. Your chances of succeeding are enhanced tremendously.

"Uncertainty does funny things to people," writes Linda Barbanel in *Registered Representative* magazine. "Some thrive, others withdraw in defeat. Don't let anxiety and frustration get the better of you. When things seem to be going haywire, one thing you do have control over is your attitude."

In *How to Master the Art Selling*, Tom Hopkins offers that if we "decide to concentrate on doing constructive things, that will turn opportunities into reality. You'll stay in your comfort zone because your mind is on doing, not on suffering."

Concentrate on doing constructive things. It's using the concept of positive thinking to change and redirect your habits by refocusing. It is not a process that will turn you into an enthusiastic zealot, promoting something in which you have only a marginal belief.

"Your clients have problems they want solved," says Ms. Barbanel. "You have to be the problem solver. If you only commiserate over the doom and gloom of the daily headlines, you won't make any sales; but if you learn of the problems your clients have, and relate to them... you'll improve your position."

One of the most difficult things to deal with in business is the "halo effect" of bad times.

The "halo effect" in good times has you basking in the reflection of another's success.

If you own the restaurant or shop next to the place where everyone wants to go or are the other act on the bill with a major hit act, you'll enjoy significant spillover success. In bad times, the same dynamic can occur. One day things are going great and sales are good. You are the owner of a company that manufactures fondue pots. Suddenly, alas, you are yesterday's fad food centerpiece. Nobody wants your product. It doesn't even rate a glance at garage sales.

And what of the fondue cookbook? It's in the back row on "the ninety-nine cents table" at the book shop, a victim of a negative "halo effect."

The definitive story on recessions has the shopkeeper doing pretty well. Business is so good, he expands, hires more employees, and business gets even better so he expands some more and hires more people and business gets still better, so... you get the idea.

One day, the shopkeeper's son returns home from the university with his brand-new MBA and shouts, "Pop! What are you doing expanding? Haven't you heard there's a recession going on? You've got to cut back and hold down operating costs before you go bust!"

So Pop starts letting people go and cuts his advertising back from six pages a day in the paper to two pages every other day, and he cuts out the free delivery stuff too. Gradually, over the next few weeks, sales are off, traffic is slow, so he closes a location, lets a few more people go, cuts advertising even more, and fires the press agent he'd hired to get stories about him in the paper. So the stories stop coming. So do more customers. The old shopkeeper slumps in a chair, depressed, and moans, "My son was right. How could I have continued expanding and never even noticed this recession?"

Once upon a time that was more funny than true. Today, the opposite is the case.

Nothing succeeds like success.

People like to do business with people who look, act, and are successful. It makes them feel confident, makes success seem contagious—a "halo effect."

People do not like to do business with losers. People who live each day with a "gloom and doom" philosophy are losers.

Market analysts note that the stock market collapsed in October of both 1987 and 1989, but the theories of why the market collapsed have only one thing in common: disagreement among the theorists. If nobody knows why the market collapsed, how do we avoid a reoccurrence? Step one is to re-read the "shopkeeper" story.

How do you avoid the "halo effect" of a recession—of having your business suffer because the doomsayers have pronounced it a bad time to buy anything?

One way is to diversify.

Note the uniqueness of your constituency and market to separate segments. Broaden your range of services to offer, say pickup and delivery at one end of the scale and discounted self-service at the other.

Charles Schwab built a successful network of "discount" brokers by advising investors that, if they knew what they wanted to buy and sell, Schwab would handle the trades for lower commissions than the brokers who gave "full service" with research, advice, and checking. It was much the same way a gas station differentiates between self-service and the more expensive full-service. Gradually, Schwab expanded to add not only full-service brokers, but "programs" for a broader spectrum of investments and investors—something for almost everybody.

Sony went from manufacturing electronics to manufacturing electronics *and* owning two movie studios and a record label.

If Rupert Murdoch's magazine sales go soft, he still has his TV network and movie studio.

RJR Nabisco? From Winston cigarettes to Oreo cookies and lots of choices in between, it amounts to putting all those eggs in a lot of baskets.

Another way to fight the negative halo is with your own separate spotlight. The more you emphasize your own uniqueness, the less you are potentially the victim of the industry negatives. For example, amid all the savings and loan failure headlines and stories, Citibank and its CitiCorp Savings increased their advertising, their visibility, and their expansion efforts to look as if they were blossoming. They were, of course, having problems of their own during the period—and they addressed them pretty well—while distancing themselves from the problems of their industry.

On this point of "spotlighting" yourself, the best way to accomplish this is to utilize the very basic elements of marketing—advertising, public relations, promotion—only even more so. Usually, companies commit "the big blunder" by going in the other direction. All their best instincts say that a strong marketing program is more important during bad times than in good, yet in bad times the belt-tightening finds advertising, PR, and marketing budgets early casualties.

Fortune magazine notes "old reflexes that used to kick in when recession loomed will have to be rethought... experts argue that smart companies will find the funds to increase advertising and new-product launches."

Harvard Business School professor John Kotter adds, "It's a different set of responses. You don't just say 'It's tough times, let's cut.' You take risks and spend more."

You want your customers and clients to trust you, to give you business, and to spend their money with you. So why would you think they'll move confidently in that direction when they see your company cutting back?

Again from *Fortune,* perhaps the most definitive summary on marketing in the worst possible time: "Probably the worst thing you can do... is to panic and, like some corporate lemming, lead your company off a cliff in the name of cost savings. The recession will end someday. If you've done little during the bad times to boost service, improve your product, or bring out new ones, you'll be way behind when the bright skies eventually dawn."

At a Glance: Timing Is Everything

Take another look at marketing strategies for "the worst possible time."

- Expect a miracle. Be optimistic. Work on your attitude. Be realistic. Be positive. Believe in what you're doing.
- Remember the basic fundamentals of effective marketing don't change because the market climate changes.
- In bad times or in good times, your plan requires: a situation analysis, objective, strategy, tactics, and realistic budget.
- Write, phone, e-mail, and send newsletters and articles. Remind clients you appreciate their business. Remember:
  - Your customer is someone else's prospect.
  - Your best prospect is a satisfied customer.
- Tell clients, customers, and prospects you are sending something to them; send something to them; call to discuss what you sent. Treat this as a service call. If it results in new business, congratulate yourself, but don't push.
- Listen to your customers and clients, and send information. Define a plan that speaks to their needs.
- Stop selling and start helping.
- Sell a solution to a problem, not just a product.
- Tell the truth.
- People believe things they see in writing. Use good sales literature, or, if needed, create your own from newspaper and magazine articles.
- Diversify. One product or service approach might not be right for everyone. Define your product in terms of its value to your customer or client.
- Spotlight your uniqueness. Advertise. Publicize. Realize that cutting your budget and lowering your profile also lowers your awareness/recognition, brand loyalty, and ultimately your sales revenue.

Part II

Creating a Marketing Strategy

Chapter 4

The Value of Market Research

What some people in business hate about market research is that if it tells them something they already know, they feel they have to defend its cost against charges of wasting money. If it tells them something that they *should* have known, but didn't, they worry about having to defend themselves for not being up-to-speed. The problem, of course, is how to deal with not doing research and blundering ahead taking risks in unknown territory.

Research has become an increasingly important component of a marketing plan. Whether at the initial stages, revision stages, or responding to market shifts—whether routine or of crisis proportions—knowledge of your target group's attitudes forms the basis of your planning.

For years market research was produced on demand to justify pretty much anything a company or client wanted to do. A study or a survey that showed "nine out of ten" people questioned would respond to whatever it was the researchers wanted was considered sufficient justification by a nervous board of directors to fund a product or program that otherwise might give them pause.

Figures could be manipulated.

Data could be skewed.

Analysis could be highly subjective.

Consider the politician who reveals that there is tremendous support for his or her candidacy, only to find little or no support after the votes are counted.

In advertising, competing brands in the same market will declare they are each "number one" "the largest dealer," or "the preferred choice."

How can there be more than one "number one?"

Because they produce the research to back it up, that's how.

In the 1980s, research became the darling of the advertising industry. Always considered essential to some, dubious to others, and to still others a necessary evil that drew dollars from media and creative budgets, the use and value of research was a topic of controversy and debate. Among the industry's rising stars were the new generation of MBAs who loved research reports that told them what people thought and bought and why. Manufacturers and marketers could make decisions with success predetermined. The great quest for knowledge had finally been fine tuned. The art had become a science, So why did products that did well in test markers or met the desires as articulated in surveys bomb? Any number of reasons:

The test group was wrong.

The survey questions weren't clear enough.

People changed their minds.

Market factors changed.

The sampling was too small.

People lied.

Firms such as A. C, Nielsen, Dun & Bradstreet, Opinion Research Corporation, The Gallup Organization, Arbitron, and others gained national respect and recognition for developing standards and procedures that assured the integrity of their surveys and studies. Still, there were those who claimed that failures following forecasts of success in market research gave the process all the credibility of *The Old Farmers' Almanac's* weather forecasts.

The late David Ogilvy, one of the most respected and often-quoted elder statesmen of advertising, notes in his book *Ogilvy on Advertising,* "Advertising people who ignore research are as dangerous as generals who ignore decodes of enemy signals."

Mr. Ogilvy strongly endorsed the process with his "18 Miracles of Research," including the measure of your company's reputation among consumers, security analysis, government officials, newspaper editors, and the academic community. Research too, he suggests, can help you decide the optimum positioning for your product as well as your target audience, and it can also help define the "promise" of your product in an ad.

In another section of the same volume, however, some 120 pages earlier, Mr. Ogilvy addresses researchers and identifies nine "bones" he has to pick with them. These include a rather diverse list of complaints from the use of "pretentious jargon" and graphs that are "incomprehensible to laymen" to taking too much time, having little or no system for retrieving research that has already been conducted, and, very significantly, being "full of fads."

It was not the first time (and surely won't be the last) that one person offered opinions that seemed contradictory.

While Mr. Ogilvy directs his concern over fads to examples from the 1960s, at no time was this concern more dramatically exemplified than in the 1980s and continuing into the 1990s. During this period the more mainstream scientifically based research organizations were joined by a long listing of what were commonly referred to in the trade as "trend shops." One of the most visible of these was headed by the author of *Megatrends,* John Naisbitt, who purported to be able to identify coming trends and advised businesses on a wide range of points including new product introductions, positioning, and packaging.

Other such firms include the Paris-based Trend Union, and Promostyle, Dominique Pechlars, and Nigel French. Lest trend shops as research be casually dismissed, note New York's Here & There shop has advised such clients as General Motors, as well as Bloomingdale's parent, company, the latter on what they predict will be coming trends in fashion, fabrics, and colors.

Few "trend shop" firms have been as influential as the consulting group Brain Reserve, whose founder, the promotionally-oriented

Faith Popcorn, reportedly receives fees of up to $1 million per project from such clients as Eastman Kodak, Pillsbury, and the Campbell Soup Company. Ms. Popcorn and her staffers reportedly read magazines, watch television, and make street, restaurant, and office observations on fashions, food, and snack preferences. Based on these observations they forecast the next coming trends for their clients.

These "trend shops" publish reports and studies that are sold to corporations for prices ranging from $1,500 for a Promostyle or Trend Union book on crystals to a Brain Reserve "Trend-Pack" that, sent to clients bimonthly for $12,000 annually, includes samples of popular foods, tapes, toys, and other consumer items.

Though trend shops might seem hard to take seriously as analysts or forecasters of public sentiment when put into the same category as established statistical market research firms, they are taken very seriously indeed by corporations around the world who pay millions for their assessments and conclusions. Many people holding doctorates or master's degrees in market research dismiss trend shops as about as scientifically reliable as Us magazine's annual list of "What's Hot and What's Not." It may be entertaining or interesting, but are such conclusions to be taken seriously as research? It's questionable.

Research, by definition, should provide information based on a statistically representative sampling of significant numbers. Research should represent conclusions. Observations of trends, fads, and opinions of a sampling should be viewed as information— as data—but to use such as research itself can be misleading and costly.

What should research cost?

That depends on what you want the research to tell you. The first step should always be to collect and review what you absolutely know about your company, product, customer, competition, and market environment. Make the distinction between what you know and what you *think* you know. It might seem like a waste of time and money to pay for something you already know, but what if the research proves you were wrong? Was it then worth the cost if it avoids an expensive miscalculation of the opinions, attitudes, awareness, tolerance levels, and preferences of your customers, shareholders, or regulators?

Too often there is a corporate reluctance to undertake research because the CEO believes he or she surely knows (or *better know*) the product or market or shouldn't be in the job in the first place—and that goes double for the vice president or director of marketing. This may be a good time to point out that a substantial number of CEOs, chief operating officers, marketing directors, and others continue to attend seminars, conferences, and trade association meetings to share information.

Can confirming what we already know, or telling us what we don't know, go too far?

Yes. To validate data is one thing; to prove the obvious, at a very large cost, can make one look foolish. An example of this is the U.S. Postal Service. Upon receiving complaints too numerous to count regarding the poor quality of service, the Post Office hired the prestigious firm of Price Waterhouse to conduct a survey. The results of the survey confirmed what the public had already known and what only those running the Post Office didn't seem to know: service was, indeed, bad. Adding insult to injury was the fact that the cost of the survey was borne by the same public which had voiced the complaint. With all due respect to Price Waterhouse and the U.S. Postal Service, couldn't they have just read and counted the complaints?

Other instances of using research to make oneself look silly are rampant in the magazine publishing business where publications with declines in circulation will frequently produce surveys and studies to suggest to advertisers that they're really doing great and it only *looks* like they're slipping. *Playboy* magazine, for example, commissioned the Roper Organization to conduct a survey that they announced earnestly "has gone a long way to erase the perception that *Playboy's* editorial is behind the times."

Advertising Age carried a report that certain men's magazines were also read by a number of women, so research would be commissioned that would help attract advertisers who wanted to reach women and otherwise would not consider men's magazines for their ads.

Oh.

Eric Miller, editor of the newsletter *Research Alert,* noted in the same *Ad Age* story on this subject that magazines pay up to six-figure sums for readership research.

"It's a lot of money for not a whole lot of return..." Miller confirmed.

John McSherry, of the Bozell advertising agency, noted that "Most media planners don't just take a publication's survey findings as the last word. In fact, many view magazine research as being self-promoting . . . [and irrelevant as] they are giving me answers to questions I haven't asked."

Few serious marketers would disparage the need for solid research, but when the result is self-promoting and answers questions no one asked, it has told you little of what you really need to know about yourself and your market, and the result is wasted money.

A marketing plan is the essential element of a successful strategy. But before such a plan can be created, the basic research must be in hand. Unless you know as much as can be learned about your market, to proceed with your plan could be somewhere between too costly and disastrous.

Look to research to supplement the definitive answers to these questions about your company, product, or service:

1. What is the potential market for your product?
2. Who is your customer? (Male? Female? Age? Income? Geographic area? Education?)
3. How much do you know about the things that are important to your customer? (Family? Religion? Politics? Patriotism? Retirement income? Health and fitness? Musical tastes? Leisure time? Sports? Safety? Environment? Children?)
4. Who is your competition?
5. How are you perceived—alone and relative to your competition? (Older? Younger? Cheaper? More costly?

Better at first, but weaker on follow-through? Continually getting better?)

6. What percentage of customers are repeat customers—yours alone and those of your competitors?
7. What is your customer satisfaction level?
8. How important are quality, service, cost, product guarantees, and the reputation of your company to your customers—and in what order?
9. Are you known to the media beyond your own advertising?
10. How frequently or extensively is your company, product, or industry the subject of media attention— favorable and unfavorable?
11. How influential does such coverage appear to be? Relative to sales, returns, mail, phone, or e-mail comments?
12. How involved is your company or industry in community, charitable, or philanthropic causes—alone and relative to your competition?
13. How susceptible is your company or industry to cycles? (Seasonal? Economic?)
14. Is your advertising effective?
15. Does your business increase significantly with the use of discounts, rebates, or seasonal price cutting?
16. Has your product or company won any awards or been recognized for something noteworthy? Has your competition? If yes, does it affect sales?
17. Are you a member of any civic associations or trade groups? Does this appear to have any impact on your business?
18. Has the growth in e-commerce benefitted your company?

The object of this exercise, of course, is to create the basic profile of your company or product, alone and relative to your competition, in your community and in your industry.

Positioning yourself in a time of crisis can be the difference between surviving the crisis or not. Positioning before the crisis can give you something upon which to anchor your plan. If the data you have collected by answering these questions shows gaps, the time to begin closing them is before your competitors or market forces can exploit them.

Few things in life are as simple as they seem. Don't be misled by the apparent simplicity of these research questions, however. For example, question 3 might seem all too obvious. After all, aren't such things as safety, children, family, health, and fitness important to everyone?

The answer is no.

- For years automobile companies installed seat belts that thousands of drivers not only wouldn't use, but openly resented. The cries grew louder when the belts were attached to buzzers.
- Junk foods outsell health foods.
- Cigarette sales are actually up in many countries of the world, while health studies and warnings intended to discourage their use get wider attention.

Don't assume that what you believe to be obvious is accepted and embraced by all. Let collected, reliable data produce the conclusions you rely on when developing your plan. Questions in your research as to whether your customers are smokers, vegetarians, are overweight or underweight, or have summer homes or pets can tell you a great deal directly and indirectly about their habits, lifestyle, preferences, and tolerance levels. These are no small considerations in determining how your customer (or community) might respond to your crisis or your attempts at damage control.

The CEO of a large U.S. advertising agency told an American Marketing Association conference on marketing research: "The new buzzword is bonding, and what is now important is discovering what bonds a person to a product."

Equally valuable is knowing why customers reject certain products. Knowledge of this type is marketing gold.

Experienced marketers know not only the value of research, but how to get it at the lowest cost. Sometimes at *no* cost.

Traditional methods of research—personal interviews, focus groups, mail and telephone surveys, location polling, point-of-purchase questionnaires, and observation—are usually costly. To large companies about to launch a major campaign to position their products or a campaign to save their product or company, the budget could be in the millions of dollars. Certainly an attempt to cut corners on gathering the information that could prove vital to the success of the endeavor is foolish. Allocate your research budget commensurate with its value to you. In many instances, however, research is available from sources close to you, through your trade association, trade media, or the business press.

American Banker, for example, publishes an annual Consumer Survey that specifically addresses the subject "What Consumers Want." The cost is modest. A portion of one survey asked fifty-eight questions, covering eight topics, of more than one thousand heads or co-heads of households of a randomly selected cross-section of the U.S. population. For any one bank to have undertaken such a survey of attitudes and opinions would have run into the tens of thousands of dollars. The survey detailed consumer sentiments on the S&L crisis, service quality, credit cards, and a number of other major issues.

The Roper Organization published an excellent study called *The Influential Americans—Who They Are, How to Reach Them*, which was sent to subscribers of Roper's newsletter *The Public Pulse* and offered such valuable information as who are the influential Americans, as well as their loyalties to specific brands, consumer dissatisfaction, hobbies, health and fitness habits, education, purchase habits, and social and political influences. While updates and break-outs are useful, this core data is extremely valuable, accessible, and affordable.

Major business publications such as *Forbes, Business Week,* and the *Wall Street Journal* frequently conduct subscriber studies detailing attitudes, as well as purchasing habits, investment portfolio make-up, and key lifestyle considerations. These and other publications do an excellent job of reporting other people's research as well. Good marketers subscribe to and read trade publications— their own and those of related industries—where studies, polls, and survey data are reported regularly.

Trade magazines provide a wealth of data on trends, lifestyles, careers, and much more relating to market research. The information in any one issue often yields useful statistics comparable to any number of expensive studies. Other people's published research is available in single volumes for relatively small amounts. Of course, it won't be as specific as you might want it to be, but so much of value is available at such low cost as to be worth investigating.

Trade journals exist in print and online for most professions and industries. Read them. Their sole mission is to offer information of value to their specific audiences, and very often industry research is the centerpiece of such publications.

Too often corporate managers and marketers will be so closely involved in their internal circles of influence that they lose site of the consumer attitudes and awareness that drive their businesses. This is a mistake that can be costly during the best of times. In a crisis situation, it can be devastating. Buy and use current research to take the pulse of your market and plan your campaigns. To do otherwise is comparable to driving at high speed with your eyes closed.

At a Glance: The Value of Market Research

- Whether your research tells you something you didn't know or just confirms something you did know, it is budget money well spent.
- Be careful of the so-called "trend shops." Their material is interesting and often fun to review, but it is not research.
- Research should provide information based on a statistically representative sampling of significant numbers.
- Research should ultimately represent conclusions, not merely reflect fads.
- Make the distinction between what you know and what you think you know.

Chapter 5

The Marketing Plan

A marketing executive was invited to give a talk on the subject "Getting the Most from Your Marketing Plan." The host group's executive director called to confirm the date and said, "I'm glad you're going to speak to us about developing a business plan."

"No," the speaker replied, "I'm a marketing guy. I'm going to speak on developing a *marketing* plan."

After a pause the host asked, "Aren't they the same thing?"

No. They are not.

The business plan is what is provided to the bank or investors and outlines what a business's product or service is, how it would be produced and distributed, the type of research and development procedures and funds needed to succeed, the size and composition of the potential market, and cost and profit projections over a given period. Based on this, the bank or investors determine that you don't have a chance of succeeding in these difficult times ... or they get out their checkbooks. Once funded, the business plan moves to the left side of the desk and the marketing plan to the center.

It's a problem that too often people don't know what we think they know. We don't want to be condescending and present a plan at an elementary level and insult anyone, but, at the same time, we must be clear at every step that all participants are clear about what's being done and why.

It's usually assumed that senior executives have a basic knowledge of marketing. The most successful executives usually have achieved their success, however, by never assuming anything.

The American Marketing Association defines marketing as "the performance of business to consumer or user."

In his book called simply *Marketing*, the University of Tulsa Professor Robert D. Hisrich expands on this, noting, "Marketing is the process in which decisions are made in a totally interrelated changing business environment on all the activities that facilitate exchange in order that the targeted group of customers are satisfied and the defined objectives accomplished."

Whew!

Perhaps something a bit more concise will suffice. Let's define marketing as the *"packaging, positioning, pricing, promotion, distribution, and selling of a product or service."*

The marketing plan is the outline for accomplishing this. Sometimes it is strategic in nature and is as brief as our definition. Sometimes it is hundreds of pages thick and seems as deep and rambling as Professor Hisrich's definition. Too often the really weighty marketing plans seem as if they were created to satisfy either someone's ego or someone's boss. They are painstakingly written, copied, bound, and placed in a drawer never to be looked at again.

The best marketing plan is one that people value and use. It's a map, a guide, a checklist that, when viewed as such, should never be so complicated it discourages anyone involved in the marketing effort from using it.

While research is a major component, both in formulating the marketing plan and in evaluating its correctness, research must never be used as a justification for inflexibility or even failure. That is, in recognizing that market factors can change in a day or in a moment, a marketing plan must be flexible enough to accommodate change without becoming obsolete or irrelevant.

Too often timid marketers rely on research alone as a justification for their decisions or, worse, their lack of decisions, to be responsive to changes in the market climate.

In *Contemporary American Marketing*, Harper W. Boyd, Jr., and Richard M. Clewitt quote Alvin Toffler's *Fortune* magazine article, in which he notes of Pepsi-Cola's never-ending, intense rivalry with Coca-Cola that while "the product varied wildly from franchise to franchise, even more serious was the fact that it was tied to an out-of-date market strategy." Do not allow yourself to be locked into an inflexible plan.

For structure, yet maximum flexibility, an effective marketing plan might take this form, considered standard by marketing professionals. It should include:

I. Situation Analysis
What do you know about your product, market, customer, and competition? This is the place to utilize your research. Consider your own history, standing, regulatory considerations, and future prospects—pro and con.

II. Objectives
"What do you expect your marketing plan to accomplish? Increase sales? Market share? Name awareness? Change public opinion? Win recognition or praise from regulators or critics? Set not only objectives, but deadlines for reaching them. Be realistic.

III. Strategy
What approach will you take to achieve your objectives? To some, the marketing plan itself represents a strategy—a strategic approach to doing business.

IV. Tactics
What will your strategy require you to do? Advertising, public relations, research, promotions, and lobbying are separate

functions, vehicles, and disciplines. They can work together, separately, or compete and contradict each other. Determine which tactics best apply to your strategic plan, identify them, be specific, and coordinate their implementation.

V. Evaluation

Measure your results. Determine if your tactics are working and on schedule. If not, determine if new tactics need be employed or if your strategy is flawed. Or both. Or neither. At this point you should again consider if your objectives were realistic or if market factors changed along the way. At each deadline point you have set, reevaluate your plan and, finally, be flexible.

What about *time*?

The period of time typically covered by a marketing plan is usually tied to *budgets*. Since advertising, public relations, investor relations, and other components of the plan can be costly, the plan should be subject to major review and revision, just as most budgets are.

Funds should be allocated for contingencies. Planning is important; evaluation is critical. In evaluating your results, you must have the funding available to alter your course. Should your advertising need to move in another direction, for example, media, creative, and production expenses can be costly. Allow for the possibilities of such changes during the period for which you have budgeted.

If your goal is to achieve certain objectives over a five-year period, for example, budget realistically, anticipating changes and inflation. Review your plan and ask what changes will be necessary if it succeeds or falls short and make projections accordingly.

In the past two decades, media and technology have undergone massive makeovers. Allow for the possibility of that happening again as you move forward, never quite knowing how radical changes might be.

Be flexible

Here Is a closer examination of the basic elements addressed by a well-defined marketing plan:

Packaging

Is your name and/or logo and signature familiar? Inviting? Suggestive of security and stability? Warm or brightly colored? Boring or bland? Is your most readily identifiable characteristic that you blend into the background? What can you do about this? What do you want to do about this?

Some companies use corporate colors extensively as a means to identifying themselves. Websites, cards, order forms, cartons, delivery trucks, service vehicles, uniforms, and envelopes all sport uniform "company colors." UPS is a very good example of this. The brown trucks and brown uniforms with the familiar shield can be spotted a block away. Federal Express has that kind of look as well, suggesting every bit as much consistent reliability as its largest business rival, the United States Postal Service. For at least a couple of generations, the dairy industry exemplified purity and clean living in its home delivery services by way of white uniformed milkmen in their white trucks, delivering white milk, eggs, and cream. The trucks and uniforms may be gone, but the concept is still viable.

How much is enough to make you familiar and friendly, a part of the lives of your once and future customers?

Pricing

How do you determine pricing of your product or service? Regulated? Fair trade? Well-promoted discounting? How is your price perceived in relation to that of your competitor? Is the value of your product obvious? Is the value reflective of the cost?

For years every ad for the candy breath mint Clorets ended with the line, "Clorets cost a little more, but Clorets *do* so much more." Whether they did or didn't do much more was not as important as the company's positioning statement and the sense of value it attempted to convey to its customers. The result was that Clorets racked up very respectable sales against its competitor, Life Savers candy breath mints, which sold for about one-third the cost of a package of Clorets.

Sometimes the pricing is beyond reasonable control. An example is the case of drug companies, where research, development, and manufacturing costs force the product to be priced high compared to what the public thinks the product should cost. The price isn't too high, it is only *perceived* as too high. The challenge to the marketer is to establish value to the customer beyond what he or she would like to pay. For years people were willing to go into debt, pay almost any fee, for the best doctor or the best lawyer or the best stereo system or car. Quality—or perceived quality—consistently won out over cheaper or generic brands. The 1990s were to be the decade of belt-tightening and sacrifice, but for that segment of the market for which quality is the only choice, the American Express Platinum Card still carries weight at better upscale locations.

Promotion

Within the broad definition of marketing, a variety of disciplines are each distinct, but interrelated, including:

- advertising
- public relations
- education
- publicity

Many people believe that public relations (PR) and publicity are the same thing. They aren't. Publicity is *publicizing* something. It may be an item planted on a blog, in a column in a magazine or a local paper, or it may be a skywriter, a handbill, or stunt. Public relations is a much larger activity that includes investor relations, government relations, scholarship funds, recognition and awards programs, informational lectures, concerts or other performances—live or recorded or media—or any of a myriad of other projects. A company's annual report is a legal and financial document, but to many companies it is also the centerpiece of a PR program. Education includes literature, seminar courses, research studies, white papers, and, most recently, the hybrid "advertorial," part education/information and part advertising, often with as much impact as the boldest product ad. The website is almost any business or organization's most viewed presentation of its image and message.

Advertising is, alone or as a component of your marketing plan, perhaps the most persuasive, effective, immediate, and expensive avenue to influence, recognition, and success. The format and media for ads keeps evolving and redefining itself, yet, at its core, it is the same, whether illustrated on a highway billboard or viewed in a video posted on a website or YouTube.

In an earlier book on advertising, I offered nine points to maximize the effectiveness of an ad program. They all relate to market research and the marketing plan and are worth summarizing here:

1. Define your market. Know who you are talking to in terms of age, sex, marital and family status, business/profession, income, and geographic influences.
2. Identify your competition.
3. Prepare a competitive analysis.
4. Determine how much your customer knows about your company and product—alone and relative to your competition.
5. Identify your customers' main source of information about your product.
6. Know why your business gets better or worse—seasonality, discounts, advertising, special sales, affinity pricing programs, rebates, or news stories.
7. Know what you want your advertising to accomplish—increase awareness, reverse a negative image, expand markets, or increase sales or market share.
8. Merchandise your research.
9. Establish benchmarks for results.

Positioning

Does your public know who you are and what you do? Alone and relative to your competition? How do they think of you? *What* do they think of you? Are you a good neighbor or a less well-regarded corporate citizen?

Marketing consultants Al Ries and Jack Trout used to be partners. In a consulting firm and in a book titled *Positioning: The Battle for Your Mind*, they claimed to have "coined the word *positioning* to describe the process of putting your brand or company into the mind of the prospect." The word and its usage carry so much power that it is often at the center of every marketing plan. How a product is positioned will affect its pricing (bargain/low-cost/mass market or top-line/big ticket/upscale), its distribution (online, discount warehouse stores/the shop at the mall/home shopping TV network or personally shown by appointment/limited quantity/exclusive franchise), and its packaging (generic/commercial or private label). The Ries and Trout book has gone through a number of editions. A subsequent volume, The New Positioning, proves that time marches on, often in new and different directions (as did Ries and Trout), but the original plan, If managed well, remains pretty solid.

Do not confuse image advertising and corporate advertising, two terms frequently incorrectly used as if synonymous. Corporate advertising is used to get the target audience to know your name, to make them aware of your presence in the marketplace—to make them think of you. Image advertising is to affect *how* they think of you. To this end, positioning might be a factor in the corporate campaign. In a corporate sense, a company or product may be "number one in the world." In an image campaign, the company would be known as the "oldest, largest, and most trusted name dedicated to your family's health and safety." The difference in the approach is between your market just thinking of the company and *how* they're thinking of the company.

As Ries and Trout noted in *Positioning,* "the basic approach ... is not to create something new and different, but to manipulate what's already up there in the mind, to retie the connections that already exist."

Your marketing plan, through your packaging, pricing, promotion, and positioning, will determine to a very large degree *that* your target audience thinks of you, that they know you're out there, and how you fit into their lives. A phrase like "the world's most trusted" is the product not of quality or efficiency, but marketing.

Media selection is important in advertising because the best ad is a waste of time if no one sees it. Similarly, the best company, service, or product is doomed to failure if it isn't correctly marketed (packaged, priced, promoted, and positioned). Some of these points seem obvious and logical. Yet so many efforts fail because the obvious is overlooked.

At a Glance: The Marketing Plan

Remember that your business plan tells your bank or investors what you propose to do, how you propose to begin and to maintain it, what you expect to achieve in terms of sales and market share, and how much money you'll need to do it. Your marketing plan, however, is the strategic map for achieving your goals.

- Be flexible enough in your marketing plan to be responsive to changes in market climate.

- Consider the elements of an effective marketing plan: the situation analysis, objectives, strategy, tactics, and evaluation.

- Remember that the basic elements of your marketing plan should consider: packaging, pricing, promotion, and positioning, as well as distribution and sales.

Chapter **6**

Determining Which Way to Go: Different Aspects of Marketing and How to Make Them Work

Very few of us are so smart that we truly believe or even pretend that we know everything. However, that doesn't stop us from telling *other people* that we know everything. In any number of corporations, the person in charge of marketing is also often in charge of advertising, public relations, promotion, and even education. Clearly there are overlaps, but there are also very distinct differences. Ideally, in a coordinated campaign, these functions support each other. In too many instances, they compete for both budget and attention. In most marketing plans, the various disciplines are singularly managed and are coordinated for greatest effectiveness.

By definition, advertising is the paid placement of your message. Whether the medium is television, radio, magazines, newspapers, billboards, point-of-sale displays, handbills, posters, car-toppers, soundtrucks, skywriters, or the World Wide Web, you are paying for and controlling your message space.

Good advertising is memorable, attention-getting, and effective. It is also, in the most effective media, relatively costly. The best advertising relies on talent in the writing, presentation, and production. Some advertisers employ well-known personalities from entertainment, sports, politics, or fashion. While more expensive, this type of advertising increases the effectiveness as well as the memo ability of the ad. Often, but not always. Consider these advertising moments that almost rate Hall of Fame status:

- Pepsi-Cola's television commercial featuring singer Michael Jackson reportedly cost more than $1million to produce. It received huge amounts of free publicity, but whether or not it caused more people to by the product has never been proved.

- The Advertising Council produced a public service television commercial showing a frying pan with an egg dropped into it, cracking and fast-frying while the announcer intones, "This is drugs. This is your brain on drugs. Any questions?" It cost a fraction of the Pepsi figure and is considered a classic example of modern, powerful television advertising.

Both commercials were very well produced, extremely effective, and memorable. Of course, much of the talent was donated for the public service spot, but the comparison is offered to show the contrast between big production and understated simplicity. When done well, both can work and both have their markets. The essence of determining what's best for your company or product, whether you are choosing an ad, media, or a marketing discipline, is quality.

A common complaint and a frequent argument against advertising is its cost. Some companies will claim they don't advertise because it doesn't work for them. Good advertising, done well, is always effective. Too frequently, the plan under which it evolved was ill-conceived and its objective not clearly defined. An image ad, for example, will gain recognition, increase awareness, and stir feelings or emotions. It won't necessarily generate increased sales during a specific time frame. If the goal is sales, it's not the ad that's failed, it's the strategy for reaching the goal and the tactics that were wrong.

Magazines are highly specialized. So are the seemingly ever-increasing number of satellite and cable television channels operating in most markets. You can now target your message to a well-defined audience with less waste than ever before and very cost effectively.

Websites, blogs and Internet ads are still in something of an experimental stage, in that some Internet ads work, most don't, and marketers haven't yet settled on a highly-likely formula for success.

Consider the strongest factors in favor of advertising:

- You select the media where your message appears.

- You control the content of your message 100 percent.

- You have complete freedom of creative control to use whatever attention-getting device you choose from celebrities or animation to fireworks or symphonies.

- You can run your ads with as much frequency as you can afford and desire.

- You control not only the media, but the day and time your message appears.

To those who suggest that much advertising lacks credibility, there's certainly some truth to that. But note those ads that refer to studies and surveys of organizations such as the American Medical Association, American Dental Association, or numerous government reports. These ads have credibility and, if done well, inform and educate as well as sell. Of course, the public understands that a spokesperson is paid for his or her endorsement, yet many are so above reproach that no one dares to question their integrity—fee or not.

One of the key factors in having advertising succeed is a *belief* in advertising, of its power to influence and its effectiveness in carrying your message to the masses. Nowhere is this more the case than in formulating a response to a crisis situation. An ad campaign that addresses the crisis can be powerful, pointed, effective, immediate, and responsive. It can also, if mishandled, be dismissed as transparent, exploitative, or manipulative and compound the damage. All good advertising—even corporate and image advertising—has a sales message. Sometimes it's hard-sell, sometimes not. The crisis ad must sell a point of view with far more integrity, credibility, and persuasive emphasis than is typically required of a single product ad or an entire campaign. The stakes are usually higher.

Like advertising, public relations encompasses many different actions and aspects. Henry C. Rogers, the founder of Rogers & Cowan, a successful U.S. public relations firm, explains "... public relations is not easily defined, even in the field. Ask a hundred public relations men or women to define their business and you will get a hundred different answers, usually abstract or obscure."

Public Relations News offers that PR is the management function that elevates public attitudes, identifies the policies and procedures of an individual or an organization with the public interest, and plans and executes a program of action to earn public understanding and acceptance.

Scott M. Cutlip and Alien H. Center, in *Effective Public Relations,* call the process "the planned effort to influence the opinion through good character and responsible performance, based upon mutually satisfactory two-way communication."

It is amazing how professional communicators can take a subject that is supposed to be essentially a simplified process of communication and make it appear complex with their array of interesting definitions. This may have something to do with the tendency to overstate. Henry Rogers, however, adds, "very simply, my job was to get the client's name in the paper."

Public relations is an area that, because it is so broadly encompassing is often misunderstood. It is ironic that this effort—

relating to one's public—is the process that is supposed to show one's best side, yet is very often viewed with suspicion. For example, during the 1960s U.S. President Richard Nixon's White House was said to be populated and controlled by PR men. This was intended at the time to be a disparaging remark, inferring PR people personified a lack of honesty.

By the 1980s the popular term in both corporate communications and government circles was *spin control* as practiced by *spin doctors.* This described the tactic of having a spokesperson follow an announcement or public appearance with an interview in which an attempt was made to manage, reshape, and define both the content and tone of what was said and influence the direction of media coverage.

Presidents Roosevelt and Kennedy were said to be experts at "managing the news." Their exclusive, friendly interviews with, and influence on, members of the news media resulted in a more favorable, less objective treatment and coverage. today they would be described as "masters of spin" -- guiding media coverage to reflect most favorably on their programs.

The PR "practitioner" may have reached the pinnacle of power and importance in the early years of Ronald Reagan's presidency when his assistant, Michael Deaver, was regarded as having the ear of both President and Mrs. Reagan, and as being closer to the couple and more influential than most members of their immediate family or the president's cabinet. Mr. Deaver was courted by favor-seekers and the media alike and ultimately left the service of the president to exploit this relationship in the corporate world. In so doing, however, Mr. Deaver was charged with selling his access to the administration. He was some-what discredited for a time, humbled, and the subject of an investigation and trial.

The same administration's press secretary, Larry Speakes, wrote a "tell all" book about his White House experiences and was criticized, as well as discredited, for violating both privileged communication and public trust. As a result, he lost a lucrative job with a nationally respected public relations firm. It was somewhat ironic that Mr. Speakes wrote that his book was an honest account of episodes in which he lied. His finally telling the truth proved to be his downfall. One professional in the field observed that it wasn't so much that he told the truth, but that he had badly packaged it for public consumption.

In the spirit of true bipartisanship, it should be noted that President Clinton went through a series of public relations assistants, several of whom were regarded as light on press experience, heavy on "image-making." Key among them were Dick Morris, James Carville, and David Gergen, whose responsibilities often came down to meeting with members of the media and beginning conversations with, "What the President *meant* to say . . ."

These are examples of where the very practice that was developed to engender goodwill came to be regarded with suspicion, distrust, and disdain. The individuals responsible were smart enough to know better. The very sense of good judgment that makes a PR person effective seemed to have lapsed in these instances.

Public relations as a broad category encompasses publicity, press agentry, corporate communications, shareholder and/or government relations, and promotions. While the functions have much in common, they are distinctive:

Publicity is simply publicizing a subject by generating coverage in the media or raising public consciousness. Publicizing rarely involves more than "announcing" to get attention and generally takes the form of announcements such as news releases, bulletins, or even town criers.

Press *Agentry* may include publicity, but goes further. The press agent works with the media to provide, present, and position a client's product or message in the most favorable light by providing background information, research, sources, and quotes. In public service, this person may be called the *press secretary* or *public information officer.* This is the person who promotes and arranges interviews and acts as the official spokesperson, the advance person, or consultant to the corporate or public official regarding the form of the interview or presentation and the specific points to be emphasized, avoided, or handled with care.

Billionaire industrialist Howard Hughes is said to have employed press agents to keep news and information about his activities *out* of the press, as he wished his privacy protected. Most corporate or public officials wish the opposite. They believe, with some justification, that positive information given to the public about them and their work will increase their perceived value, particularly in relation to their competitors or rivals.

In advertising, the truism is that if you're a better *known* product or company, you are perceived **as** a *better* product or company. The press agent aggressively addresses the goal of getting the product or company better known.

Corporate Communications is normally a function within larger companies where objectives are twofold: internal to the corporation's employees (policies, directives, newsletters, closed-circuit TV programs, reports, videos); and external (to vendors, consultants, suppliers, and others who interact with the company via newsletters, books, magazines, videos, policy directives, surveys, or studies).

Shareholder or *Investor Relations* is concerned with producing and circulating annual and interim reports, financial data, prospectus material, studies, and literature that provides existing and prospective investors with the legal and other types of valuable information to help them make the most informed investment decisions. While the Securities and Exchange Commission requires that certain information be provided to investors, often a report generated to satisfy regulatory requirements serves also as the corporation's "showpiece." Many are elaborately designed, engraved, embossed, printed, and bound and contain upbeat letters from chairpersons, presidents, or founders with lush photographs of the corporation's best and brightest people, facilities, products, and its most optimistic forecasts. This material is mailed to shareholders and investors, as well as distributed at meetings and presentations. It is additionally offered to financial editors and writers, securities analysts, brokers, and other investment representatives in mailings, meetings, presentations, breakfasts, and luncheons in printed form and on slides, videos, charts, and so on to generate the maximum favorable interest. These annual reports commonly have a six-figure budget and even go on to win awards. There are competitions for "best annual report" and a good PR person will, if such an award is won, exploit that fact as a reflection on the company's skill at communicating effectively with its shareholders.

In the period prior to the 1960s, many investor relations people were lawyers or accountants, strictly charged with the preparation and dissemination of financial reports. Others during the same period were referred to as *stock touts*. Their responsibility was to generate interest or persuade stock analysts at major brokerage and accounting firms to write favorable "letters" or recommendations of the stock. This latter practice fell from favor, became regarded as disreputable, and largely ceased to exist as it left an unsavory impression, suggesting that if a stock had to be promoted door-to-door like sample laundry detergent, it must not have much going for it. The investor relations person today primarily disseminates news releases and announcements of new offerings, dividends, splits, acquisitions, mergers, and profits and losses that present the company honestly and in context. Analysts and editors know what questions to ask and what to look for and these PR professionals know what to provide and how to provide it. The essentially promotional breakfasts and luncheons may still take place, but are presented as question-and-answer sessions, where the presence of a CEO and the price of a meal is in no way considered an inducement to write a favorable recommendation. Indeed, rather the opposite. The members of the audience, both the analysts and media, are more sophisticated and wary.

Governmental Relations is the area of public relations whose members are more commonly referred to as *lobbyists*. Their function is to attempt to influence government officials who will enact laws or regulations that will enhance or restrict their clients' business practices. Lobbyists are usually lawyers or former government officials. Most large public relations firms have offices in capital cities through which clients retain these practitioners to plead their case. Like the spin doctors, lobbyists have a mostly dubious image as a group. Usually, the public is offered an image

Important Questions and Answers About Our Recall.

Ford Motor Company
Dearborn, MI 48121

T. J. Wagner
Vice President
Customer Communication
& Satisfaction

To Our Ford, Lincoln and Mercury Owners:

As a responsible company we feel an obligation to our customers to address their concerns, which is why Ford Motor Company recently announced a program to voluntarily recall 8.7 million vehicles to replace ignition switches. While the actual number of complaints was less than two hundredths of one percent of that total, it is important to us that these concerns be properly addressed.

Q: What happened?
A: Following an intensive investigation in cooperation with the U.S. National Highway Traffic Safety Administration and Transport Canada, we determined that the ignition switch in a very small percentage of certain models could develop a short circuit—creating the potential for overheating, smoke, and possibly fire in the steering column of the vehicle. The factors that contribute to this are a manufacturing process change to the ignition switch in combination with the electrical load through the switch.

Q: What vehicles are affected by this voluntary recall?
A: The following model year vehicles are affected:
- 1988 Ford EXP.
- 1988-1990 Ford Escort.
- 1988-1992 Ford Mustang, Thunderbird, Tempo, and Mercury Cougar and Topaz.
- 1993 Ford Mustang, Thunderbird, Tempo, and Mercury Cougar and Topaz models built prior to October 1992.
- 1988-1989 Ford Crown Victoria, Mercury Grand Marquis and Lincoln Town Car.
- 1988-1991 Ford Aerostar, Ford Bronco full-size sport utility and Ford F-Series light truck.

Q: What should I do?
A: If you own one of these vehicles, you will receive a letter from us instructing you to take your vehicle to the Ford or Lincoln/Mercury dealer of your choice and have the switch replaced free of charge. However, you do not have to wait for our letter. You may contact your dealer and arrange to have the switch replaced immediately if you choose, free of charge.

Q: How long will it take?
A: The repair procedure should take a little less than an hour. But please contact your dealer in advance to schedule a time that is convenient for you; they are making appointments daily. We have already completed about 300,000 appointments.

Q: What if I need additional help?
A: You may contact your dealer anytime, or call our Ford Ignition Switch Recall Customer Information Line at:

1-800-323-8400

With nearly 5 million ignition switch repair parts already available, we are ready to address your concerns immediately. We'll take a major step like this to make sure that people who buy a Ford, Lincoln, or Mercury vehicle know that they bought more than a vehicle, they bought a company and a dealer organization that stands behind the cars and trucks they build and sell. That is our *Quality is Job 1* promise to you. Thank you for your patience and support.

Ford has had its share of recalls, exploding gas tanks, and bad luck on wheels, but this ad came early enough and was well-conceived enough to reinforce the existing goodwill built up over the years for the company that already had America's best-selling car. They could, however, have done without the somewhat self-righteous opening line "As a responsible company…"

of the lobbyist as someone who lavishly entertains senators, congressmen, and regulators and attempts to ingratiate themselves with glamorous trips and the use of private planes, yachts, villas, etc. Despite continuing murmurs and demand for restrictions and reform, this still happens.

The much larger group of lobbyists, however, meet, present their case, and follow up much in the manner of any competent sales representative. Granted, the tobacco industry has a strong "lobby" to make certain their positions are well considered before legislation is enacted, but so do those representing their opposition. Veterans' groups, teachers, senior citizens, and the handicapped, as well, have representatives pleading their cases. The practice is legitimate and some would even describe as honorable. It appropriately employs people and methodology to bring a message to the attention of a target group in an attempt to influence decisions. Unfortunately, scandalous conduct by some lobbyists caused perceptions of the entire profession to be tainted and suspect.

Frequently, corporate management will choose public relations over advertising based on cost factors alone. The most powerful ads aren't powerful at all unless they are seen and that means buying media that is costly. Public relations, it is often argued, is cheap exposure. The PR person is paid a fee, usually a fraction of the typical cost of print or electronic media ads, and presents a story idea to writers, editors, or producers who take it from there: free TV time or print space for what may be anything from a "mention" or an "item" to a profile, article, segment, or even an entire program.

All true.

But consider this: advertisers control their space. No one interrupts or offers an opposing opinion of the advertiser's message. Not true with PR. Once a story idea has been presented, it's open season. The editor or reporter might use your information, but might also include comments from everyone on the planet who has ever had a negative experience with you. This is done in the interest of fairness and "objectivity."

Further, your story might run in the least favorable space or time from your point of view, and you have no control over it. It is not your space to control. Unflattering photos might be used. So might even more unflattering quotes. And about those bargain rates, consider that, at the time of his death in 1978, public relations pioneer Benjamin Sonnenberg, almost always referred to as "the influential New York publicist," liked to tell friends he had earned somewhere between $15 million and $30 million in his professional lifetime. If that figure is an exaggeration, it isn't by much.

PR giant Hill & Knowlton, in one of its more controversial moves, was retained by the United States Catholic Conference to represent the group in its battle against abortion rights organizations. The agency's fee in this instance was an estimated $3 million to $5 million. Their total revenue from PR fees in that same year (1989) was $168 million. And that was not a freak year. Good, competent public relations services can be every bit as costly as a good ad campaign, The Catholic Conference could have done a fair amount of advertising with the same $3 to $5 million and controlled 100 percent of the space where the ads appeared. Offsetting this is the impact a favorable story carries when wrapped in the framework of the morning newspaper or evening TV news. The very format of the presentation provides weight that paid ad time or space rarely can match.

One further area to note is that of promotions, again a facet of the marketing/advertising mix. Promotions, when called *sales promotions,* meant putting your logo on premiums, such as T-shirts, key chains, coffee mugs, caps, and bags. When used in this way, nothing much has changed in the promotions category, except that items once given away free are now often sold. However, when the goal is to build consumer trust, such promotions as a free trial offer, in-home service, money-back guarantee, *double* your money-back guarantee, extended service warranty, free exchange privileges, free pick-up and delivery service, no charge for credit, discounts, or trade-ins are effective. In a crisis situation some of these may work well within a campaign to rebuild trust. Promotions can be a highly cost-effective add-on to a campaign. For lesser known companies, it is "soft" as a central or primary marketing vehicle.

So, to maximize the impact of the marketing plan most efficiently and cost-effectively, is the best route advertising or public relations (with or without the various branches or categories aimed at investors or government)? It depends on the objective of your plan.

Advertising offers tremendous impact and immediacy. PR provides the credibility of the news or feature press, but you sacrifice control over form, timing, and, most importantly, content. The objectives in your marketing plan will, to a large degree, dictate your strategy and tactics.

At a Glance:
Determining Which Way to Go

The "Advertising vs. Public Relations" chart that follows makes a summary argument for advertising, public relations, or both. Remember that there are other avenues of marketing and carefully consider which best fits your marketing plan;

- **Advertising**
  Does it fit your budget as well as your marketing plan? Where should your ads be (TV, newspapers, radio, magazines, billboards, direct mail. online)?
- **Public Relations**
  Is publicity enough? Remember the wide range of PR vehicles available, from newsletters to brochures to bill stuffers to annual reports.
- **Corporate Communications**
  Communicate your message effectively to your own people and to those with whom you do business. They are the ones who carry your flag every day.
- **Shareholder or Investor Relations**
  As with your staff, loyalty and support should build from within and those who have invested in you deserve to be kept informed and can be utilized in visible demonstrations of support, if needed.

- **Promotions**

  Caps and T-shirts can engender affection and a sense of team spirit, but the other promotions—free delivery, extended warranty, 10-day/no obligation examination, etc.—suggest service, integrity, and quality. Don't overlook either side.

Advertising vs. Public Relations: Either or Both?

Pros and Cons

Advertising

- + Total control of message space
- + Total control over choice of media, program environment, and time of exposures
- + Sense of immediacy
- + Bright, dazzling, memorable, creative
- - Acknowledged bias as audience knows it's paid space
- - Public predisposition against ads (people say they hate commercials)
- - Usually expensive when done right
- - Could be even more damaging if crisis response message is not well constructed

PR

- + No charge for media exposure
- + Message not constrained by a 15-, 20- or 30-second time purchase or a small space
- + Carries greater impact and credibility if reported as news
- + Larger sense of "personal involvement"
- - Cannot control content of what is reported or presented or when
- - May be disadvantaged in sharing space or platform with opposing message
- - Could take a totally negative slant
- - If negative, will likely have a long reprint/rebroadcast life

Chapter **7**

Marketing Ethics— In or Out of a Crisis

When a company—and perhaps all you've worked for—is under fire and on the line, was there ever a better time to believe that the end justifies the means?

Was there ever a more legitimate time to allow for a certain ethical leeway?

No.

You're either ethical or you're not. You cross the line or you don't. Expressions like *pushing the envelope* are created to somehow make it seem as if the rules have changed about what's okay. The rules haven't changed. The attitudes of the players might have.

Very often business is its own worst enemy. An *Advertising Age* study notes that "consumer rancor toward big companies climbed rapidly in the 1970s, moderated through most of the 1980s, and appears to be on the rise again. The Exxon Valdez oil spill, insider trading scandals, the savings and loan debacle—all may contribute to the stunning 80 percent of Americans who think 'most big companies are just out for themselves.'"

Consider these headlines, referenced in a presentation on "Business and Social Awareness" in the publication *Conscious Choice:*

"PUSH Asks for Boycott of Nike"

"Alaska Spill Cleanup Behind Schedule, Senators Say"

"Executive Calls Federal Recycling Standards a Fraud"

"Pentagon Investigates Widespread Contractor Cheating"

"Savings and Loan Costs to Taxpayers Could Reach
$2,000,000,000"

"Companies Dump Dangerous Products in Latin American
Markets"

If the headlines aren't bad enough by themselves, business's track record for compounding mistakes seems to be reaching new heights. The P. T. Barnum line about there being "a sucker born every minute" doesn't carry much weight in the high-tech, global communications age. If people are slow to catch on, that only gives business time to prepare for the anger and bad blood that follows. The consumer, to put it mildly, is angry and is going on the offensive.

Patricia Katherine Novick, a Chicago-based therapist, wrote "Every day, headlines... challenge Americans to face the complex issue of corporate social responsibility. In a society where governmental power is at least presumed to be circumscribed by checks and balances, the latitude allowed to companies is great, and the mechanisms for limiting that latitude... are weak. Many companies have established charitable foundations or other means of donating money.... A business that exploits workers or pollutes the environment, and then donates to the local opera company cannot be said to be acting responsibly."

It comes down to ethics, personal and professional—and to integrity. Some people touched by scandal might be exonerated, but they carry the baggage forever. They might as well have been guilty for all the good being innocent does them. Yet, others seem to lead a charmed life. Almost.

- Ford Motor Company had so much customer goodwill that the failure of the Edsel was laughed away and the Pinto's exploding gas tanks were largely forgiven. No one ever thought the Ford Foundation was a do-gooder ploy to distract public attention from the company's problems. The public wanted Ford to come through all right.

- Continental Bank in Chicago followed a series of bad business decisions with a federal bailout. It was on the brink of ruin, but astute management and public sentiment helped put it back on track. The public wanted Continental to make it, and regulators and creditors were willing to cooperate.

- Archer Daniels Midland was charged with price-fixing and agreed to a fine in the nine figures. Without missing a beat, the huge agricultural conglomerate donated to presidential and congressional campaigns and played a visible role as an active, involved, good corporate citizen. Do we wonder why the public shows signs of cynicism?

- President Clinton won reelection by a substantial margin. Yet, a large percentage of voters said they did not trust the president but would vote for him anyway. What then is the message being sent to others in public and private life about standards of acceptability?

People claim they are mad as hell and are not going to take it anymore! Yet, they *do* seem to keep coming back for more of the same. They are disappointed and disillusioned with business, government, education, law enforcement—all the established institutions—yet they still want them all to succeed. Most of them anyway. The alternative is unacceptable.

Boxing champ Mike Tyson went to prison for raping a young woman, came out of prison, resumed his career to cheering crowds and earned millions. Tonya Harding, implicated in an attack on a rival skater, was not sent to prison, yet was banned from ice skating *for life.*

In business, sports and entertainment, politics, and government, the standards of conduct and ethics seem to be getting lower and the public is becoming more resigned to it. Underlying all, people still express a desire "to do what's right."

How might business respond to public distrust and cynicism? Honestly.

The basic set of guidelines that helped build countries and companies and somehow, for some reason, was set aside is still workable. Ethics, honor, and integrity built reputations, and reputations generated business that built companies and careers. Of course, all the business factors must be in place (the product, service, price, convenience), but people keep coming back and supporting companies when they believe in them and their products.

The Johnson & Johnson Tylenol case is the classic example, but certainly not the only one. An airline's worst nightmare is a devastating air disaster that not only takes lives but could spell the end of the company. Airlines fail because of poor management or bad business decisions. A horrible crash doesn't deter most people from flying a particular line because people want to believe in the company, its people, and its commitment to safety.

Ethics in the marketing department is a reflection of ethics in the executive suite and at all other levels of company management. A company, product, service, or person regarded as ethical is one people trust. We see the interrelationship of honesty, integrity, quality products and services, respect for consumers, and a dignified profile builds trust—a topic we keep coming back to—a trait that, all other business factors in place, could cause you to succeed and without which you might more easily fail.

If you are better known, you are perceived as somehow better. If the way you pursue becoming better known is through an ethical, high-visibility presence, you create and solidify a good reputation. That reputation is better than gold in good times, but most especially so in times of crisis.

It has been noted of advertising that the best ads are worthless if no one sees them. Similarly, it is important to demonstrate the ethical commitment you've made to your position. It seems, in a way, sad that anyone would have to make a public display of something as basic as honesty and ethics—something that should be simply assumed to be the case.

Alas, it isn't. To create and nurture your public image, your integrity must be visible. Make it visible. Here are some recommendations:

- Whether a product or service, a guarantee suggests quality. A money-back guarantee suggests quality and commitment. A double-your-money-back guarantee means that you are willing to stand behind your product or service to the fullest possible extent.

- "Truth-in-advertising" became a cliché suggesting that, if not required to be truthful, advertisers would lie. Few lied. Many exaggerated. If you can't tell the benefits of your product truthfully and generate business, you obviously have a weak or flawed product and your problem is not one of marketing.

- The cousin of the truth-in-advertising warning is mis-representation. That is, the insurance company's recruitment ad that asked for "public relations trainees." Yes, they would in fact be "relating to the public," but what they wanted were people to sell life insurance, a very challenging and not always prestigious endeavor. The attempt to "glamorize" the job was not just shameful, but suggested the company didn't put much value on its own profession, much less its product. There will be a lot fewer complaints and lawsuits if we simply tell people what it is we want, expect, and are willing to accept.

Similarly, the sweepstakes that advises "you may have already won ..." has in the smallest possible print "along with seven million other possible entrants." Again, if the product or service has value and quality, it should be the focus of your message. Prizes for trying a product or sitting through a pitch are a nice touch, but if someone has to be lured into your presentation, they will likely be weak prospects or the first to show buyers' remorse, exercise a guarantee option, and back out.

The worst offender in this "lure them into the pitch" genre is the direct mail piece that appears to have come from a government agency. Brown, window envelopes with a quasi-official looking return address, similar to those used by the Internal Revenue Service or the Department of Defense, and that contain a letter or form with very "official" looking type and copy and disguise the proposition— even the product—are despicable. Usually, of course, these types of promotions are for products that even the company recognizes are hard to sell. Given that, the products are camouflaged. Companies using this approach are usually not terribly interested in recommendations for ways to be more visibly ethical. A borderline misrepresentation case is the highly controversial *infomercial,* usually a thirty-minute television program that takes a news or talk show format, but is actually a product information presentation (thirty-minute commercial). The Federal Trade Commission has received numerous complaints from viewers who charge they've been duped. Regulation or legislation is frequently suggested to protect the unsuspecting public.

Consider: any attempt to trick or mislead the consumer through your marketing is not only bad marketing, but speaks horribly of your company. *When,* not *if,* problems result, both the public and industry regulators tend to be less than sympathetic.

Infomercials can be very powerful sales vehicles. There is no reason to use them to mislead your prospective audience/customers/ clients unless you don't think your product has enough going for it to sell on the basis of its merit.

Clearly identify that the infomercial is a pitch for your product or service. If people are interested, they'll watch and buy. If not, they won't. If you somehow lure them into watching by suggesting that the program is a news, talk, health, or business program they will likely resent it—and you. If for some reason they do buy, they are prime candidates for returns or, at least, dissatisfaction. There is no reason to mislead. People do watch product videos at point-of-sale setups. People also call or write for product videos on health and fitness, investments, sports, hobbies, and dozens of other subjects. Advertising supplements in magazines and newspapers get read without disguising their purpose. Advertorials in newspapers are clearly advocacy ads. The public recognizes this and responds accordingly, usually with respect for the integrity of a person or company willing to put its name on something.

Making a video, whether a three-minute music video, thirty-minute infomercial, or two-hour movie, is a creative challenge for the writers, directors, and performers. Give them this challenge and let them go.

The story of OxyWhite tooth whitener, if it's a persuasive story, doesn't have to be disguised as "Superstories with Lyle Waggoner," and David Kibbe's beauty makeovers can be interesting to audiences of prospective customers, rather than being packaged as *Talk of the Town* starring Shelley Hack. Marketers don't need to "fudge."

A good product and a good story well told is the whole point of a marketing and advertising program. When the story is told with integrity it helps the sale along and builds brand equity and loyalty.

At a Glance: Marketing Ethics

Ethics isn't part of the corporate promotion package, it's a nutrient that runs through the bloodstream of your business.

- Be credible.
- Be honest.
- Take credit for the things you do right—from cause marketing to community service to fair trade and fair employment practices.

- Take responsibility when things go wrong and set them right—whether it's a missed delivery, a bad trade, or an oil spill.

Your constituents will forgive and even respect people and companies that exhibit honest and honorable behavior. Ultimately, of course, this is just good business.

Part III

A Crash Course in Crisis Marketing

Chapter 8

The Marketing Process in Brief

It might be an oddity that among the most popular books read and quoted by senior managers in American business at the end of the twentieth century are books on "The Art of War" as taught by respected Japanese warriors and written in the seventeenth century. The psychological implications and symbolism are rich: *business/ war, American/Japanese.*

In a presentation on crisis marketing, we can easily make a case for offering the wisdom of the undefeated dueler, masterless samurai, and independent teacher Miyamoto Musashi, written, in 1643, in what has come to be regarded as an extremely important text, *The Book of Five Rings.* Consider how directly these rules of the warrior apply to the challenges of today's business crisis:

1. Think of what is right and true.

2. Practice and cultivate the science.

3. Become acquainted with the arts.

4. Know the principles of the crafts.

5. Understand the harm and benefit in everything.

6. Learn to see everything accurately.

7. Become aware of what is not obvious.

8. Be careful even in small matters.

9. Do not do anything useless.

The second half of the twentieth century began the "Age of Specialization."

We were looking at new opportunities—for careers, for investment, for entertainment, for a quality of life. Virtually every category now has a list of subcategories: home entertainment is not just a television or radio, but a video recorder, DVDs, plasma screen TV, and notebook computers; dining out can be the most elegant cuisine or drive-through fast food, with much that falls in between where, regardless of our choice, our order will be entered, our bill calculated, and change determined by handheld computers.

Of the original "three r's" of education, only reading must still be done without the help of a computer. For now.

Clearly, this new order has presented both opportunities and problems. Dr. Marvin Cetron, president of Forecasting International, predicted that while the number of lawyers in the United States reached nearly a half million in 1995, the fastest-growing career position was that of paralegal assistant—the lawyer's basic support person. Between 1985 and 1995 the position posted 98 percent growth, more than double that of comparable positions in the health care and financial services industries. Lawyers and their assistants have a disproportionately high employment growth statistic because virtually nothing in modern life is not in some way covered by laws, from the content of preservatives in the food we eat and the minimum amount we can earn, to the speed we may drive and so on. One of the things the law allows is that virtually anyone can sue almost anyone else at anytime.

And they do.

Even exercising one's "freedom of choice" seems ultimately to end up in court, with smokers' rights challenged by non-smokers, environmental protection suits, and charges of misleading or fraudulent claims over products or services.

Perhaps the most notable case reference in this volume is that of the Exxon *Valdez*, which is likely to be in court for many years to come. Maybe the world would have been a better place had cooler heads prevailed and the matter of a disastrous oil spill could have been resolved by the perpetrator merely cleaning up the mess, apologizing, and compensating those whose homes and businesses were adversely affected—by "doing the right thing," so to speak.

But that's not the way it works.

On another page we note Kellogg's claim that its breakfast cereal would reduce the risk of certain diseases and the Texas attorney general's office didn't believe them, so it was off to court.

Quaker Oats had a similar problem.

Religious fundamentalists have at various times charged that letters on a Pepsi can spell "sex" and that Procter & Gamble's man-in-the-moon logo was a concealed Satanic symbol.

The lawyers were looking into it.

So, for the marketer who is about to face another day, hoping and praying that he or she will be allowed to market products and services on the basis of their quality and value without being defensive or having somehow to repel an attack, the odds, alas, are not in your favor. Here is a basic outline—a crash course—in steps to follow before, during, and after a crisis situation is upon you:

Before a Crisis:

- The Basics: Know all you can know about your company, products, market, and competition through attitude and awareness research.

- Create a reservoir of goodwill.
  1. Make your job and your career a personal matter. Learn all you can about what you can do to enhance your value to your clients or customers. *Listen* to your market.
  2. Establish value. Skip the self-serving claims about being the biggest and the best. Show and tell the benefits of your product or service in advertising and personal communication. People want to know "what's in it for them." Tell them.
  3. Write to people. No matter how large or small your operation is, your constituency always takes note of and appreciates being remembered personally, even if the communications are "personally" computerized. Large mailings are fine for what they do, but whether a broker, insurance representative, talent agent, salesman, or CEO, a personal note sent to clients, media people, or other business professionals will get read and be remembered.
  4. Take and return phone calls. If people are to give you their business, they deserve your attention on some level. Even if an assistant handles the communication, keep in mind that people remember how they are treated—and they tell *other* people about it.
  5. Be responsive to inquiries, complaints, and comments.
  6. Be a good listener. Listen to your constituency: customers, staff members, regulators, and media covering your industry. One of the greatest goodwill devices is to let people know you heard them. Remember to distinguish between listening and waiting to talk.
  7. Communicate. If you have sales material, brochures, surveys, studies, endorsements, or reports, use them. If you don't, clip articles or columns from newspapers and magazines and send them to people who will

both benefit from the material and remember your thoughtfulness in sending it. A Midwest executive rarely sees an article in one of the business magazines that doesn't make him think of someone he wants to share it with. Such ripped-and-mailed articles have come to be identified with him among his business associates, who think well of him and speak well of him whenever they get the opportunity to do so.

8. Don't assume that because you haven't heard about a problem there isn't one. Routinely make "service" checks by phone, letter, or e-mail. And always remember that your customer is someone else's prospect.

9. Show confidence and knowledge—and humility. Most people who inspire confidence in others demonstrate confidence in themselves by being knowledgeable and informed and sharing what they know. They also avoid becoming full of themselves. Arrogance in business is dangerous; in a crisis, it is deadly. Be calm, confident, and natural.

10. Do good and do well. Be a good corporate citizen. Sponsor local groups (sports, the arts, youth programs, events for seniors and less fortunate people in your community) and identify with a high-profile cause that will enhance both your visibility and goodwill among your constituents. Be sincere. If you're only identifying with a cause for public relations value, your participation could well appear transparent and opportunistic. Recognize that there truly is value to you in "doing good" in your industry and community.

11. Think positively. Position positively. Expect to do well.

- Identify yourself by your good name.
    1. Increase awareness by having a name people can recognize and appreciate. Let it be something that tells people not just who you are, but what you do.

For every IBM, there are a thousand alphabet and acronym-named companies that don't mean anything to anyone. In crisis situations it is valuable to have a good name to trade on.

2. Build brand equity. Generic may be cheaper, but the public wants a name they trust—a name backed by a reputation.

- Build trust.
    1. Be honest. Don't exceed credibility in claims or ads.
    2. Advertise. It is sometimes costly, but is inarguably the "cost of doing business" and the "price of success." Advertising works and very good advertising works even better. Let people get a sense of who you are and what you represent in a space you totally control.
    3. Use public relations effectively. Publicize what you do in news releases, bylined articles, and position papers, and host lunches, breakfasts, and round-tables. Sponsor events that will help increase both your visibility and public image.
    4. Position your company or product. Don't let others define your place in the market.

During a Crisis

- Designate a single spokesperson.
    1. Don't confuse both the subject and your constituency by bringing out the CEO, lawyer, PR chief, and celebrity spokesperson. Have a designated individual represent your position and issue updates in a timely manner.
    2. Don't let your spokesperson upstage your message. Occasionally, a company will bring in a well-known former government official, a retired military figure, or an admired broadcaster or journalist to act as spokesperson, on the idea that such an individual's

Integrity would not be questioned. Does it help the cause or prove to be only a brief distraction from the problem? A prominent, respected individual or a "power name" should support your message, not overshadow it.

- Tell your story first.
    1. A primary rule of crisis management (after "be honest") is *be first*. Get your story out before someone else does—perhaps the media, a competitor, or a critic. By being first, you have an opportunity to set the tone of the coverage and establish your openness and candor. Not being first with the story will frequently force you into a defensive or "reactive" position that is rarely a favorable one.
    2. Be prepared. Have statements ready, preferably with written handouts, and anticipate a worst-case scenario. Hope it doesn't come, but be ready.
    3. Never go "off the record." The term is great, but the actual situation has a long and glorious history of getting people into trouble. If you don't want information to be attributed to you, don't say it.

- Position your product or company in a larger context than the crisis.
    1. Offer brief statistical data from your research bank noting good things you've done—especially if those things received past media attention. By presenting as much positive information as you can, the crisis isn't minimized, but it is shown as not being all that people know about you. Tell how long you've been in business, how many customers you've served, awards you've won, and jobs you've created.
    2. Cite your participation in causes, in your industry, and in the community. Draw upon your reservoir of goodwill.

- Keep your own people informed.

  1. Don't leave your employees with only what they read in the papers. You owe them more than that. As a former PR expert explained, "The key to resolution of the problem may lie with employees. The ability to respond to a... disaster and resume operations is likely to depend on the support and commitment of the workforce." Whether the nature of the crisis is a natural disaster, a scandal, a bankruptcy, or a questionable ethical situation, your ability to survive and recover is based in no small part on your own team and how they support your handling the situation.
  2. Keep your workforce "on the team." Let them know what's going on, but ask that they not speak out publicly individually. Again, lawyers like to minimize a flow of information and comments through containment, but you cannot expect loyalty and support when you leave your own people subject to the embarrassment of their not knowing what occurred and your position on it. Conflicting or half-informed comments, though well-meaning, can seriously hurt the effort. A regular series of e-mails and postings to keep the Information flow consistent and on track becomes currency in bad times.

After a Crisis

Repeat all the steps noted under "Before."

1. By knowing your market, who comprises it, and what they want, you will be in a strong position before, during, and after a crisis. Strength comes from what you know and knowledge is power.
2. Advertising, public relations, and a full-fledged communications program should be a part of every business's ongoing

program—large or small. Such programs define both that people think of you and how people think of you. They position you within your industry, your local community and perhaps the global community. Given their level of importance, they should be major line-items on every agenda and operating budget.

4. Have a sense of humor.
5. Be honest.

At a Glance:
A Crash Course in Crisis Marketing

Sometimes even the smartest people in corporate America mess up. Charity and sensitivity often seem to have gone with the 1960s. It's a pretty safe bet that when corporate America messes up, lawyers and special interest and citizens' groups will be ready to exploit the matter. Business must be ready too.

Crisis marketing requires a positive attitude—expecting to succeed when things look their most bleak. It also requires honesty. Don't embarrass yourself or your company by getting caught in a lie. Spin control, looking for ways to make black appear white, or outright misrepresentation will most assuredly come back to bite you. To say that you can't discuss something at this time is okay. Lying is not okay.

Some people—mainly lawyers, actually—have suggested that crisis marketing with its emphasis on public relations is a cosmetic solution to a very serious and costly problem. Sometimes, however, cosmetics are all you've got to work with. Covering over a blemish won't make it go away, but it won't make it worse and, just as important, it won't cause it to spread to someone else. Just as some people will not walk out the door until they are properly dressed and made up, don't let your business "out there" without it being "properly dressed."

In our high-tech business environment the challenges are greater than ever, but so are the potential rewards. There are people lurking "out there" whose income is derived from suing companies. There are professional agitators and "crisis manufacturers" whose personal agenda is to attack business as a way of getting sufficient publicity and attention to heighten interest in and promote their other interests. The tabloid press has never worried much about the truth or about damaged or ruined reputations. Similarly, television shows that practice "ambush journalism" (60 *Minutes, Prime Time—Live, Inside Edition, Hard Copy)* have little interest in showing a balanced picture when one side is more juicy than the other and can be highlighted by unflattering pictures as the camera attempts to catch the shifty-eyed business executive with a bead of perspiration on his or her upper lip. Few people fare well in tabloid stories, print or TV. The stories always tend to be sensational and unfair. That's why it is important in a crisis situation that you *have a plan* and stick to it.

It has been noted that some look at a crisis as an opportunity—to use the visibility of the crisis to one's advantage, to increase market share, etc. Crises, by most every corporate standard, should be avoided if possible. Anything so unsettling is rarely good for business. Yet, serious marketers know that each new situation is a challenge to be met and a crisis is not the end of the world. Companies such as McDonald's, Johnson & Johnson, and Pepsi seem to be able to deal with their crises and win a greater public respect when the dust settles.

If your job is marketing and you see the storm clouds gathering, you'll do the job because it needs to be done. A great piece of advice on the subject is "The way you do it is just to do it," or to quote Mark Twain, "Always do right. This will gratify some people and astonish the rest."

Part IV

The Crisis Marketing Casebook

Chapter **9**

The Difference Between Right and Wrong—in a Crisis

The old salesman always liked to remind the troops: (1) Tell them what you're going to tell them, (2) Tell them, and (3) Tell them what it was that you just told them. People with marketing titles try to be somewhat less repetitious, but not by much. Two points that have been presented in this volume, but bear repeating are: (1) We live in a time of instantaneous global communication, so just as you might find your company, product, service, or yourself an "overnight sensation," negative news may travel just as fast; and (2) *Crisis* is a relative term.

Here are some cases of companies that dealt with crisis situations very well... or not very well. Hopefully, we can learn from their examples.

A Person, Product, and a Brand Named *Trump*

When a person becomes a product, then a symbol, then a brand, so that eventually the market can't tell where one ends and the other begins, it's a worthy subject for examination. Many baby boomers who came to positions of prominence in the 1980s distinguished themselves by raising indulgence to almost an art form. The media labeled them *the me generation,* and no one personified the type more than the real estate mogul and ubiquitous celebrity Donald Trump. In a book subtitled *When Bad Things Happen to Good Companies,* where does a case study of a *person* fit? Well, not all business enterprises are the size or scope of General Motors. Sometimes the company in question can be embodied in a single individual—who only *thinks* he's the size of General Motors.

Donald Trump made himself larger than any of the number of companies he ran. In effect, he became the "enterprise" from which his various companies seemed to grow. Typically, one might capitalize on high name recognition by emphasizing the quality and stability that the name stood for. Mr. Trump, on the other hand, focused a disproportionate share of attention on himself, rather than on his various businesses, which had little or no relationship to one another. Originally introduced to the public as a successful real estate developer, at his peak Mr. Trump was fronting hotels, casinos, an airline, and a board game, as well as claiming to be the creator of a TV game show— which also bore his name—and later hitting ratings success with a television "reality" show called The Apprentice, it which he bellowed at teams of young people who were competing for a job in his organization by whatever devious or dubious means they might devise.

Rather than claiming he built great companies, he preferred to focus attention on himself as an artful dealmaker and a celebrity for celebrity sake. He was the quintessential role model for would-be tycoons. What set Mr. Trump apart from the pack was his shameless pursuit of publicity and the media's willingness to accommodate him. Clearly, he made some great real estate development deals, but so did a number of other prominent individuals whose wealth was greater and whose empires more sprawling, though they pass among the general public unnoticed. People don't know their names. Mr. Trump, however, *wanted* people to know his name. He called press conferences regularly, planted stories In the media, judged beauty pageants, made sure his marriages and divorces were news, and gave interviews to announce his deals and opinions, each one touted as the biggest, most Important and most meaningful of its kind. *Ever.* He put his name on each deal—Trump Tower, Trump Plaza, the Trump Shuttle, Trump Castle, and so on. He licensed the use of his name to a board game manufacturer, a TV game show, and a marathon race, the Tour de Trump. He "wrote" heavily promoted books extolling his talent for making deals.

And then, it seems, as the expression goes, the wheel fell off. The story has been widely reported that Mr. Trump supposedly overextended himself, misrepresented his wealth, got into trouble with his banks and other creditors, missed some payments, and had to humbly seek refinancing. This all took place under the intense media spotlight that he had so zealously sought for years. Suddenly this self-styled mogul was being dismissed as a grandstanding, fast-talking salesman who had built his business on exaggeration and sleight-of-hand. The press that had indulged him now seemed to delight in recounting his problems. His only comment on his fall from grace was that his detractors should watch him, that he would be back bigger than ever—and he would even the score.

While most wealthy figures guard their privacy, Donald Trump complained to the media that he was really worth a lot more coverage than they were reporting. The general consensus grew to be that if Mr. Trump's empire were to go down in flames, few people would feel much sympathy for his plight.

Typically, lenders and investors are not very supportive of one whose business is being compared in the national press to a house of cards.

After a series of refinancing maneuvers with his creditors (who largely took the position that it was better to bend their own rules to work with Trump in hopes of making good some of their loans to him, than to close in on him and be cited for having the bad judgment to be publicly conned) Trump came back, louder and more brash than ever, but now regarded as a parody of himself, a vain, self-promoting figure who seemed like he was a character made-for-TV.

How might Mr. Trump have avoided some of the problems that had beset him? To put it simply, he could have been a little "nicer" and perhaps a little less full of himself when out in public. He might have tempered his flamboyance with a dash of grace and humility. He fancied himself a master manipulator of the media, and it appears he was. Bankers were more than willing to loan him money on his signature alone, based on cover magazine stories extolling his vast wealth and holdings, not on his financial statements.

Did the Trump Shuttle fail because it was never positioned and promoted as an efficient business travel service, or because it was merely a prop—a winged-tribute to Trump himself?

Perhaps if lodging at the Plaza or the Tower in New York City had been represented as elegance and value, service and good taste, rather than as a center of garish pyramid-like show business attractions, more people would have been inclined to take a closer, more serious look.

Playboy was never able to extend its magazine's image of sexy sophistication far enough to attract guests at its hotels, at least partly because corporate and business travelers seemed self-conscious about staying at a hotel with such a seemingly frivolous "party" image.

Conrad Hilton warmly welcomed guests to his hotels; Bill Marriott left cards in his hotels' very tasteful rooms, humbly thanking guests and asking them to rate the service and offer suggestions for improvements. The people who ran Hyatt and Sheraton took a similar approach. Mr. Trump swaggered through his lobbies, entourage in tow, easily being mistaken for one of the celebrities whose company he sought.

If there were a "Trump Foundation," a "Trump scholarship," or a "Trump shelter" or school, they were well-kept secrets. With such undertakings, public sentiment and goodwill might have enveloped him during his times of crisis and generated an outpouring of business and support, as well as respect. In testament to the power of PR, Donald Trump was reported to be important because he told people he was important enough times they believed him.

"Be nice" as a crisis management strategy? It's certainly cost-effective and easy to implement and just simple enough to be useful. It wasn't that Trump's properties were poorly run, it was that the returns were not sufficient to meet his massive debts, and the response seemed to be a position of arrogance and an out-of-control ego. Mr. Trump's creditors refinanced him and put him on a budget, rather than watch their investments crash and burn. He was again regarded as solvent, though his outbursts of bravado are often met with a yawn and coverage is relegated to items in gossip shows, columns, and websites, not the covers of newsweeklies. The lesson for the me generation is that nothing lasts forever.

Dick Morris: Crisis? What Crisis?

Not everyone in a business with his or her name on the door and reputation on the line is working on the level of a Donald Trump. Sometimes the business in crisis is a sole proprietorship—a talented individual in any of a number of professions. Perhaps he or she is a lawyer, family therapist, travel planner, accountant, insurance agent, or in some branch of the performing arts. Just as an airline, a bank, or the head of a large charitable organization might be the subject of rumors or a hostile press, so too might an individual. We know that the treasured word-of-mouth advertising (now termed "viral marketing") can help build a business, so it naturally follows that word-of-mouth can hurt and that the damage can be more swiftly accomplished if the subject is a single, easily identified and located target. Just as with the big guys, a round of negative stories can put an individual businessperson out of business very quickly.

In recent years a number of newer professions have gained considerable attention—to a large degree because of people who epitomize it having carefully sought it.

One such glamorous and often lucrative practice is that of political consultant. The job itself has actually always been around. As long as there have been campaigns, there have been campaign managers and advisors—generally some exceedingly bright manager or brash know-it-all who tells the candidate what he or she must do to get elected. These folks evolved into increasingly more sophisticated and credible professionals, dealing with polling data, demographics, psychographics, and a superior understanding of how to use the media effectively. Some of these consultants, such as James Carville, Paul Begala, Lyn Nofziger, Michael Deaver, Roger Ailes, and Ed Rollins, become as well or better known than the candidates they were hired to help elect. Often cast as spokespersons or "spin doctors" themselves, they appear on radio and TV talk shows, give interviews, and routinely write books about their experiences. Then they set out on national tours to promote the books and raise their profiles and sense of importance even higher.

Clearly one of the most successful and best known political consultants of the 1990s is Dick Morris. To qualify as "best known" it is necessary to move from the "insider" list to the front page of newspapers and magazines, often photographed when and where the client is not.

Mr. Morris helped a young Arkansas politician named Bill Clinton regain his standing—and the governor's office after an embarrassing defeat in a bid for reelection. Years later, when it looked like *President* Clinton's first two years in office left him poised for defeat in the next election, it was Dick Morris who was credited with managing a strategic makeover and a turnaround that saw the candidate coming from far behind to take the lead over his strongest opponents, eventually going on to reelection by a very respectable margin.

Between the campaigns of Governor Clinton and President Clinton, Mr. Morris was retained by numerous other candidates as a consultant. Despite his close identification with the Democrat Mr. Clinton, Dick Morris's clients were mostly Republicans. They included Senate Majority Leader Trent Lott and the outspoken, controversial, almost mythical Senator Jesse Helms. The fact that Mr. Morris became the "hired gun" for both Democrats and Republicans was frequently criticized by members of both parties as showing a lack of commitment to a particular issue, cause, or philosophy. It also clearly positioned him as, above all else, an effective professional who offered his knowledge and talent for hire, much as a lawyer or doctor might be brought in on a case solely to get needed results, not to embrace any philosophy.

This situation presents the proverbial double-edged sword. The appearance on the scene of a well-known consultant brings attention, publicity, and all of the negative associations that the consultant has accumulated over the years as well.

The choice of a consultant can sometimes announce the possible direction of the campaign. Perhaps one or more of the consultant's previous clients engaged in so-called negative campaigning and won the election. Should the public assume that by retaining the consultant now, the current candidate is likely to use such tactics? It's a fair question and not an unimportant one. A major responsibility of a campaign team is to define the candidate and his or her agenda as soon as possible—hopefully, before the opposing candidate can begin defining the candidate and forcing an image to emerge formed not by a program, but by response and reaction.

In the hiring of a celebrity endorser to do product ad promotions and commercials, a basic rule is to not select a celebrity who is better known than (and may upstage) the product. Similarly, a slick, experienced consultant who is a familiar interview guest and a high profile presence on the circuit may well be compared to and overshadow the client/ candidate.

Dick Morris handled this aspect of the process very well, cultivating his *reputation,* quietly taking a lot of credit for his clients' successes, but giving few on-the-record interviews and allowing even fewer photographs of himself to get out.

In 1996, he was riding a wave of glory that seemed to assure him continued high standing in his profession. He was being credited with the apparent near-certain victory of an American president whose image had been spectacularly resurrected. It was at that point that Dick Morris abruptly resigned from the president's campaign team.

A prostitute with whom Mr. Morris had been keeping company for quite some time had sold her story to a supermarket tabloid newspaper, having it then picked up by more respectable city newspapers. It was TV news's main story for several weeks.

A frequently asked question was, "How can one who counsels others—and people in power positions—stay within the lines and exercise caution in the nurturing and maintenance of a public image screw up so badly?"

Stupidity? Not likely.

Arrogance—a feeling of somehow being "above it all" and, as such, not bound by the same rules as everyone else? Maybe.

A couple of things are certain, though:

- times have changed and
- the best defense may indeed be a strong offense.

In an earlier time, only a couple of years actually, the consultant's client/candidate would have been scorched by the fallout from the consultant's action. In this instance, the candidate appeared totally unaffected by the news.

Some said it was because the candidate had been positioned to anticipate and withstand "character attacks" of which this, in a sense, was one. He'd surrounded himself with people of questionable morality and values, which made a statement about his character and judgment. Others said that since the candidate was not directly a participant in the consultant's scandalous acts, it was the consultant's own problem and the candidate should not be blamed for someone else's indiscretion. Still others said that the entire matter was a reflection of the times. It was simply how people behaved in the 1990s and was not all that big of a deal, that America had grown up and would not choose its leaders based on whether or not members of the leader's staff fooled around.

The consultant, in an earlier time, would have been washed up. One newspaper story detailing a major impropriety would have driven him into exile, hiding out on the island of Bimini, his career over—certainly not returning calls from the national press.

Dick Morris defied all convention.

He capitalized on being on the covers of virtually all of the national news magazines as well as the scandal sheets. He met with reporters outside his home and had breakfast with editors (and advertisers) of the *New Yorker* magazine. As if just for good measure, he signed a book contract for a campaign memoir for an amount reported to be somewhere between two and four million dollars. When *Time* magazine published its traditional "election special" issue, a guest commentary was written by... Dick Morris.

So much for the old tradition of going quietly into that good night.

What was Morris up to? When conventional wisdom held that he should be lying low, he was moving about, acting as though nothing of an embarrassing nature had happened. One might speculate that he was treating himself strategically as he would one of his clients:

- Prepare a strategy,
- Confront your accusers,
- Answer questions that allow you to position your life and work as far more significant than this minor lapse.
- Acknowledge your situation,
- Apologize for any embarrassment that may have fallen to others.

He did not, however, admit to any wrongdoing and in a rather respectful, direct, tactful manner seemed to be saying to the press and the public "Oh, *grow up!*"

How did the strategy work?

Short-term, he played it correctly and capitalized on the apparent shift in public mores, the division between those who will always be outraged and those who believe that human nature is what it is and holding public figures to standards above reproach is unrealistic.

His book will received an enormous amount of publicity and enjoyed healthy sales, if only from the curious.

Mr. Morris obviously asked himself, at some point, "what's the worst thing that could happen to me?"

The answer was: not much—only that he might be forced to find another line of work. Yet, his constituents apparently felt that his weakness of judgment in matters of the flesh did not lessen his skill as a political consultant. He had committed no crime, held no office he disgraced, had basically behaved badly, but in the social context of his times, his behavior was not uniquely.

Longer term, people will always associate his name with unsavory business and question his moral judgment.

When the upper echelon of our culture, from political leaders to members of the royal family, are involved in marital and sexual indiscretions on an international front-page scale, the antics of a political consultant seem pretty insignificant. Mr. Morris appeared to be counting on that and, at least for the near term, called it right.

Did public cynicism increase at least In part because of this incident? Yes.

Should Dick Morris have publicly apologized and disappeared from public view? Perhaps, but in all likelihood, his absence would have resulted in rumor and innuendo and made a *big* story an even more *sensational* story that could have gone on and on. It would appear that his early, calm confrontation of the story took much of the sizzle from it and caused the media to move on. The larger question of whether or not the consultant's behavior would cast a negative shadow over his client is this: the candidate's opposition will use it; the public won't care.

The Corner Gas Station and a Tale of Two (or More) Oil Companies

Anything involving automobiles seems to end up being an important story. Cars have redefined the way people live. Individuals and entire societies depend on, adapt their lives to, and evolve their cultures around their cars.

An overstatement?

Consider that the collapse of the *nuclear family In the late twentieth century* was blamed on the car. Once generations lived under the same roof or down the block, but the *mobile* society that evolved from individuals having cars allowed the freedom to buy that little starter house on the outskirts of town. You could live wherever you pleased and still be able to drive to work, visit the family, or shop at the mall on your way to the drive-in movie after a stop at the drive-in restaurant or the drive-through window or ATM at your local bank. What does a car mean? Drive-through everything: fast food, carry-out restaurants, film developers, dry cleaners, super highways and tollways, insurance, financing.

General Motors, for decades the largest automaker, was, for many years also the largest publicly held U.S. company. The effects on the environment will be considered elsewhere, but for purposes of this example, no one disputes that not only have cars determined how we live, but the direction of business. Despite the proliferation of home-based business, personal computers, and the "information superhighway," a primary consideration of many new enterprises is that they be accessible by car and have ample parking. Speeding tickets, parking tickets, and towing constitute a huge revenue base to many municipalities.

Cars are powered by gasoline and since the introduction of the personal or family car, the gas station has been a virtually unconscious fixture in everyone's life—the *friendly* gas station.

Like cigarettes, many people could never tell one brand of gas from another and convenience of location usually determined brand choice. But, like cigarettes, some people do have their preferences and brand loyalties. The oil companies know this, cultivate it, and seek to expand brand loyalty with friendly service, free or discounted car washes, snacks and soft drinks, rest rooms, litter bags, maps, and the mother of all brand loyalty builders, the credit card.

Have a Union '76 credit card? Then you'll likely drive the extra mile past the three other gas stations for the convenience of using your Union '76 card. Ditto for Shell, BP, and the rest.

The major oil companies knew that with price and quality pretty much on an equal level, the brand's image of service, friendliness, and the little extras push customers from one station and brand to another --at least that's how things worked for about a half-century.

Until the 1970s and the first of what was to be a series of oil crises. As usual, a few politicians and pundits said they'd predicted it, but mostly, the news always seems to creep up on the public and hit suddenly.

There was a shortage of oil, the people were told.

Gas station premiums stopped.

So did the free window cleaning, oil checks, and tire pressure checking.

Stations closed early.

Long lines formed.

Prices soared… and then soared again.

Americans were told that the country would have to develop an *energy policy* and an *energy program* that would reduce or eliminate dependence on foreign oil, specifically, oil from the Arab countries of the Middle East.

Friendliness at the local gas station became yet another memory of bygone times, replaced by uncomfortable defensive greetings that would continue for years.

The news media made the terms "oil company windfall profits" and "gas price hikes" and "gouging" everyday terms.

Consumers became resentful and angry. People had become programmed to a way of life that included dependency on the automobile and it ran on gasoline and they had no choice but to buy at whatever price the oil companies set.

True, the Arab oil "cartel" was the big villain, but consumers wanted and needed someone closer to home to take out their frustrations on.

Congress caught some heat for not having set up a system that protected consumers from "oil bandits." But politicians have historically led the way in buck-passing so the brunt of public ire fell on the oil companies. No free gifts or windshield-wiping was going to make up for soaring prices.

Newspapers railed with accusatory editorials. Citizen groups picketed corporate headquarters.

For once, "Shell's Answer Man" didn't have an answer.

The problem was exacerbated by the "end" of the crisis. It

seemed, after months of shortages, early gas station closings and ten-gallon limits on purchases, as soon as the price per gallon reached a certain point—in some cases double what it had been— there was suddenly all the gas anyone wanted. Stations went back to their old "open all night" schedules with no purchase limits. The already suspicious public became more suspicious of oil company pricing and practices.

And what, separately and together, was the oil industry's response to the whole matter?

Pretty much, nothing.

Despite angry charges and threats of greater controls and limits, the industry went on with business as usual, counting, it seemed, on short memories to prevail.

Some noticeable changes occurred at the pump level: customers were offered a choice between "full service" and "self-service." Full service meant you got what you used to get for the price of your gas. Self-service meant your cost was a few cents less per gallon if you pumped it yourself, checked your own oil and tire pressure, and cleaned your own windows. Cash purchases saved money again as credit card sales were rung up at a higher price.

Some gas stations, where the price was over a dollar a gallon, stopped showing prices in terms of "cost per gallon" and began showing "price per liter," which further confused many customers. The friendly gas station now posted signs explaining their "pricing structure."

Customers took it. They had no choice. The option of getting rid of the family car in favor of highly inconsistent, only sometimes predictable public transit systems and inconvenient commuter schedules won few converts. In some areas, car pooling generated interest, but not much.

A person's car was not only his or her transportation, it was a status symbol. This was true, furthermore, at every social and lifestyle level, from the luxurious Cadillac to the solid all-American Chevrolet to the smallest Toyota. And they all ran on gas.

"Oil barons" were compared to the Old West's "cattle barons," mercenary, lacking in social conscience, and suspected of bribing

Mobil advertorials, such as this one, have been appearing weekly in newspapers for some twenty years. They continue to be noticed, get read, get people talking, and reinforce the company's leadership role on issues that affect its industry, as well as America. In terms of both style and substance, the campaign and its approach have been consistently excellent.

politicians. Industry spokespersons talked of costly exploration and depletion allowances, but made few new friends. Still, the prevailing sentiment from the oil industry appeared to be to keep a low profile and wait for the crisis to blow over.

It never actually blew over, but as long as the options were so limited, businesses within the oil industry both survived and grew.

Soon the oil companies were advertising again. What were they saying?

Not too much.

Shell's Answer Man returned to remind people to check their tires and watch that anti-freeze level.

Texaco, Union, Atlantic Richfield, and Exxon continued selling gas and saying little. Only one oil company proved a notable exception both during and after the crisis: Mobil.

The Mobil Oil Corporation, believing the public was getting a one-sided picture of the oil industry from news coverage and special interest groups, decided to do the opposite of its competitors. Mobil came out—guns blazing—with a series of "advertorials." These were paid ads, formatted to look like traditional newspaper editorials, which ran regularly in major U.S. newspapers including the *Wall Street Journal* and the *New York Times*. Headlines and text demanded to be noticed and read. They were bold, opinionated, even combative and irreverent. Consider these examples:

> America has the world's best highways.
> And the world's worst mass transit.
> We hope this ad moves people.
> —The *New York Times,* October 19, 1970

> Is the energy shortage over?
> Not by a decade... or more.
> —The *New York Times,* September 5, 1974

> Caution: Too much antitrust could harm the economy's health.
> —The *New "York Times,* July 26, 1984

Partnerships: enhancing our natural heritage

Because the oil industry and many environmentalists have been at loggerheads for so long, some readers will find it counterintuitive—even shocking—to see a major oil company sponsor an advertisement for a major conservation group. What could have brought about such an unusual pairing?

Actually, the reason is simple. For 45 years, The Nature Conservancy has pursued its biodiversity protection mission by conserving ecologically important lands and waters. In the course of this work, the Conservancy has come to appreciate that economic activities such as oil exploration and development are both necessary and inevitable.

The relevant question for environmentalists, therefore, is not *if* development will occur, but *where* such activities will take place and how they will be conducted. In turn, this means that conservationists must work in partnership with natural resource companies and other interests that have a major influence on the landscape.

This focus on building partnerships with people and organizations that are making economic use of the land has produced a strong record of conservation success for The Nature Conservancy. In the United States alone, the Conservancy has purchased or otherwise protected more than 9 million acres of ecologically important land; its efforts in Latin America and the Pacific have helped conserve more than 40 million acres abroad.

Despite the great progress that the Conservancy has made, however, daunting challenges remain, and the conservation organizations cannot overcome them alone. That's why the Conservancy believes that it is more important than ever for conservationists to develop alliances with private-sector partners. If conservationists want to have a meaningful impact over the long run, they must harness the power of the market to advance both economic and ecological goals.

To this end, the Conservancy is pursuing dozens of experiments in high-priority places around the world that are exploring the potential of compatible economic development—partnerships that allow for habitat protection *and* economic growth. These initiatives include efforts to promote sustainable forestry practices in locations ranging from North Carolina to Papua New Guinea; partnerships with local farmers to prevent soil erosion and protect aquatic habitats in Ohio, Virginia, Tennessee, and Indiana; and cooperative land-management arrangements with ranchers to improve rangelands across the American West.

The oil industry has also embraced the partnership approach. For example, the Conservancy's Tallgrass Prairie Preserve in Oklahoma supports more than 100 operating oil wells that coexist with a herd of 500 bison. East Texas, meanwhile, is home to a nature preserve where the Conservancy acquired the surface rights and Texaco retained the mineral rights. And Mobil recently donated 2,400 acres of land in southeastern Texas to the Conservancy to help preserve one of the last viable populations of the endangered Attwater's prairie chicken.

Through these efforts to assure both economic and ecological vitality over the long term, the Conservancy hopes to help instill a stronger conservation ethic in the American people. Such an ethic not only respects the beauty of nature, but also values the essential role that a healthy environment plays in each of our lives.

So as we celebrate our national heritage on this July 4, let us also remember to salute our *natural* heritage—the rich diversity of plants, animals, forests, rivers, and prairies that lie at the root of our prosperity. We owe it to ourselves, and to our descendants, to be wise stewards of this bounty.

To find out how you can join The Nature Conservancy, write us at 1815 North Lynn Street, Arlington, Virginia 22209, or visit us on the Internet at http://www.tnc.org.

John C. Sawhill, President and CEO

The Nature Conservancy

A little long on text, but a solid advocacy ad for the Nature Conservatory that earns Mobil Oil "good citizen" points for donating the space to run it.

In 1980, in an advertorial under the headline "Yes, $2 billion is a lot of money, but..." Mobil hit the issue of "windfall profits" head-on, claiming "...our profits are not excessive in relation to what other companies in other industries earn on investment... Our profits and more are being used to finance the development of more energy the nation needs so badly."

In 1981, with a now typical gloves-off advertorial titled "Won't they ever learn?" Mobil hit its critics with the charge that "once again newspaper readers across the country were recently presented with a massive dose of misinformation on oil industry taxes."

In 1996, Mobil donated the space normally reserved for its advertorial in the *New York Times* to The Nature Conservancy, a major national conservation group. Under the headline "Partnerships: enhancing our national heritage" the message was clear: one of the world's largest oil companies was putting its concern for the environment first in a show of responsible business positioning.

Such placements have consistently received media attention and attracted public interest. Typically, a corporation under attack might issue a statement to respond or dispute charges, but never has a corporation so boldly stood up to its attackers, detractors, critics, and opponents and bought ad space enough to tell its story, unedited, directly to its public on a regular and consistent basis for more than 20 years.

Indeed, under the headline "Gasoline: Is the price right?" Mobil wrote, "Every year as spring moves to summer, news stories of rising prices at the gas pump appear, reminding the public again of how fickle oil prices can be. Implicit in many reports is the notion that the oil industry somehow controls the price of crude oil and thus can manipulate gasoline prices." The date of that ad copy was April 18, 1996.

And Mobil didn't stop with buying and filling newspaper space. Copies of the advertorials were sent regularly to legislators, media opinion-makers, and others of influence.

Speakers were dispatched across the United States, addressing groups of all ages in virtually any forum, often on radio call-in shows, taking phone inquiries from members of the public, most of them angry about oil prices and profits. Mobil always managed to receive credit for its courage to face a hostile public and answer questions for the record. Brochures and advertorial collections were created and widely distributed.

While this bold advocacy campaign was going on, the company was moving aggressively on other fronts. Each week public television audiences heard that the presentations of numerous cultural and entertainment programs, including the highly acclaimed series *Masterpiece Theater,* was "made possible by a grant from the Mobil Oil Corporation."

At the same time bookstores and publisher's racks were spotlighting "America's favorite travel guide series"—the *Mobil Travel Guides.* Hugely successful, these paperbacks each focused on a different region of the United States and offered "facts and specific information about where to stay and dine, what to see and do, and how to get there... even special discounts and Mobil Travel Guide I.D. cards worth up to 50 percent off on attractions and up to $10 off on lodgings. Savings can amount to $150 or more!"

And the company's Mobil Chemical Company produced a line of consumer home products carrying the Mobil logo. These included the very successful Hefty trash bags.

Mobil was putting its name in your home and your car in items from biodegradable garbage bags to travel guides to the highest quality television programs you were likely to see. At the same time they were building a reservoir of goodwill, of public confidence, by buying newspaper space to put in writing their version of where profits were invested and how much money they made relative to other corporations. The company was repeatedly singled-out for its willingness be responsive and provide information and documentation aggressively and candidly.

In contrast to Mobil's high profile and openness is its oil industry competitor Exxon and surely what is regarded as the greatest illustration of what *not* to do in a crisis.

In 1989, the Exxon *Valdez* oil tanker caused what has been termed perhaps the greatest environmental disaster of the century—perhaps *ever*—spilling more than ten million gallons of oil into the Bay of

Valdez, Alaska. The disaster in itself was incomparably horrendous and Exxon's handling of the situation seemed to make it worse.

It was clear the matter would be the subject of controversy and litigation for years to come, so it is understandable that Exxon's lawyers would instruct their client to be less than forthcoming in discussing it. However, at the same time the company was choosing to be less than forthcoming, it appeared quite comfortable placing blame for the matter with the tanker's captain.

So that was the strategy: make the captain the scapegoat and move on?

But it's not quite that simple.

Exxon management apparently not only sought to take itself off the hook for responsibility in the matter, but to cast itself in the roll of victim, suggesting "our safety practices have been excellent and we have drilled them and drilled them into our employees over the decades. There is a lot of pride in Exxon all over the world and that pride is being challenged. We'll win it back, but we're not going to do it by debating on TV with some guy who says 'you know, you killed a number of birds.'"

In the book *We're So Big and Powerful Nothing Bad Can Happen to Us,* Ian Mitroff and Thierry Pauchant note "buck passing is one of the most prominent characteristics of Exxon's culture."

Quoting an article in *Fortune* magazine, they offer "[Exxon] has repeatedly underestimated public reaction to the spills and contrives to talk as though the public has nothing at stake."

This type of arrogance appeared typical of the company as noted in their press releases. The company clearly was ready to blame its captain and the state of Alaska, but was unwilling to concede its own corporate role in the disaster. Mitroff and Pauchant suggest, "Exxon's blaming of the *Valdez* accident on one man acted both to diminish the overall responsibility of Exxon as a company and to divert attention from such threatening questions as the virtual impossibility of operating large oil tankers at sea with complete safety."

The apparent crisis management strategy: explain away the incident—the captain of the tanker had an alcohol problem. It's all his fault. Next case.

But real-life disasters are rarely so easy to explain away. Tornados, floods, and earthquakes perhaps, but ten million-plus gallons of oil pouring from a tanker whose owners had curtailed precautionary measures because the risk-to-cost ratio didn't seem to justify them, was not to be so easily explained away.

The disaster was so far reaching that a judge refused to allow a settlement by which Exxon would have paid some $100 million in criminal fines and $1 billion in civil damages on the grounds that the amount was not enough considering the extreme extent of the damage and Exxon's negligence. The public's outrage over the matter never really seemed to hit home to the company or its managers, who apparently still regarded themselves as good guys.

By the summer of 1996, the matter was far from forgotten or out of the news. The *New York Times* reported "In a stinging rebuke to the Exxon Corporation, its chairman and its lawyers, a Federal judge has held that they had all been part of an 'astonishing ruse' to attempt to manipulate the jury that awarded $5 billion in damages to pay the victims of the Exxon *Valdez* oil spill of 1989."

The judge charged that Exxon had acted as "Jekyll and Hyde" by "behaving laudably in public and deplorably in private." The company was accused of not only trying to avoid responsibility for the incident, but of entering into secret agreements that would allow it to receive a percentage of the awards it was required to pay.

Exxon's response? The company said it believed that "the court's analysis is legally incorrect."

If we are to look at this matter against any type of a reasonably standard crisis management checklist, it would seem Exxon consciously did the opposite of what have come to be regarded as fairly standard procedures when responding to a crisis of major proportions—and kept on doing so for years after the incident.

[Author's note: When originally preparing this material for publication, both the Mobil Oil Corporation and Exxon were contacted for their input and comments. Mobil responded to questions in a phone interview and sent material overnight to support its position, as well as offering to be of assistance if anything else was needed, and thanking the author for his interest

in their activities. Exxon did not accept or return phone calls and did not answer written requests sent to the company by mail. so it is no small irony that on November 30, 1999, Mobil and Exxon, two oil companies regarded by many industry critics as perhaps the best and the worst, merged... with Exxon as the controlling company.]

7 Rules of Crisis Marketing
That Exxon Should Have Followed (but didn't)

Rule One: Get your comment out first—and fast.

They didn't. The company had to have known of the disaster early and could have been out with the first, or at least an early, statement of concern, announcing that an emergency situation existed and that they were working on containing it.

Rule Two: Show concern.

They didn't. Even the clumsiest politicians remember to express concern for casualties and injured or grieving families. Exxon in this case went even a further step backward. Since the "casualties" here were fish, birds, water, and the Alaskan coastline, the company treated the early announcements with an attitude of detached indifference. After enormous pressure was put on Exxon and it was forced to pay some $2 billion toward area restoration, the haughtiness of the company continued.

Rule Three: Pledge cooperation.

They didn't. Their only concern seemed to be about their potential financial loss. While It's okay to worry about that, It's not okay to worry *only* about that. Many early accounts of containment and clean-up efforts might have been contused or contradictory, with Exxon expressing just the smallest amount of concern troubled environmentalists and the most casual observers all over the world. Further, their attempts at a clean-up seemed lazy and half-hearted, announcing they'd made some progress at wiping up the spill and were leaving, would be back in the spring to do a little more work on it—all this while film and photos showed a still black, slick beach and coastline littered with shinny black, dead fish. The biggest public relations disaster—and certainly insult to the people of the region—was the Exxon threat to sue the state of Alaska… which it ultimately did. This proved to be a capital example of a strong offense turning strongly offensive.

Rule Four: Take responsibility.

They didn't. Exxon owned the tanker, employed the crew, boasted of its skill and safety procedures, yet, when disaster struck, they sought to distance themselves from the incident by blaming the matter on the captain—specifically inferring he had a serious drinking problem—and trivializing virtually every aspect of the aftermath. Exxon's arrogance throughout the matter suggests it would like the world to believe that somehow the Alaskan coastline attacked its tanker.

Rule Five: Tell what you're doing about the problem.

They didn't. Presumably they believed their lawyers' astute predictions of long and complicated litigation and accepted that the less said, the better. Vague references to the company "investigating" lacked conviction and credibility when viewed in the context of the whole matter.

Rule Six: Discuss the crisis in a larger context.

They didn't. There were no references to the numbers of tankers inspected at regular intervals or numbers of times by objective testing or manufacturing inspectors; no reference to years of training and numbers of seasoned professionals with a combined hundred years of experience and commendation; no reference to the company's historic reverence for and dedication to the preservation of wildlife and the environment that would make such an incident out of character for the company and shocking that Exxon-of-all-companies would ever be the likely villains in such a situation.

Rule Seven: If wrong, apologize.

They didn't. As simple as it seems, public opinion—and litigators—seem not to want to banish from the planet wrongdoers who apologize and offer to make restitution, preferably before being ordered to do so.

What might this giant of companies have done to respond more positively to its participation or perpetration of the worst ecological disaster of our time?

- They could have admitted a horrendous disaster had occurred and that they were working with any and all government and private agencies and groups to bring it under control.
- Immediately impanel (before the government did) a blue ribbon group of scientists, marine biologists, and other acknowledged experts (not associated in any way with the company) to study and produce a report on the cause, the extent of the damage, and recommendations for both the necessary immediate corrective measures and programs necessary to prevent a repeat occurrence in the future.
- Announce the establishment of a grant to fund wildlife and marine life preservation, restoration, and assistance.
- Announce that no effort or expense would be spared to assure corrective action. Commit all resources of the company to this end. Note such possible responses as transporting personnel from major cities with high unemployment, to assist in the clean-up effort and containment.
- Designate an articulate spokesperson to acknowledge the legal problems, but otherwise go public with comments, answers, and reassurances to stockholders and the public.

Such recommendations are very costly. So are punitive damages in litigation, in this case running into the billions of dollars. Courts and juries are less inclined to punish a company that has already made a significant commitment voluntarily to take very costly corrective measures.

Further, the concept of creating a reservoir of goodwill, as noted in the review of cause marketing, seems to be one totally eluded Exxon management. Consider how Mobil put its name in the home on Hefty bags, vacation guides, and public television, and heavily promoted such products as its Mobil One motor oil for greater savings and efficiency. All the consumer advertising was friendly and service-oriented. And the very important advertorials told customers, stockholders, the government, and the public who they were, what they stood for, and how they were not about to allow anyone else to define their corporate profile.

It is inconceivable that if the Exxon *Valdez* had been the Mobil *Valdez,* the situation would have been handled in the same way. Mobil likely would have demanded the world judge them in context and, as good corporate citizens, conclude they were not mercenary, insensitive, indifferent profiteers prepared to walk away from a disaster with a shrug.

Exxon publicly shrugged. And compounded its public image problem by appearing to be trying to "pull a fast one" on the jury deliberating the matter.

A further consideration is the question of: is the corporation represented by management alone or everyone who works for it? If the latter is the answer, and it should be, then Exxon chose to rebuff its own family members as well. This would have been a time for all those from telephone switchboard operators at corporate headquarters to service station attendants in the neighborhoods of the world to put on a positive, community-spirited effort to make people believe that they really weren't such bad people. While, of course, individually, we should assume that typical Exxon people were nice folks, they were left as much offended and in the dark as the rest of the world at a time when a simple "public relations 101" approach of putting employees out in public to say "this is a great company—they care about people and the environment—they don't do things like this."

They didn't.

A simplistic approach?

Perhaps.

Could it have hurt?

No.

Could it have helped?

Probably.

Exxon, of course, is not only still in business, but remains an enormously profitable operation. In fact, in 2008, the company posted the largest profit ever recorded in American business—and during yet another "oil crisis.". By any standards, it has been a company in a crisis situation for years. Nevertheless, people need oil and Exxon has a lot of it. On an economic and business level, it remains competitive and viable. Indeed, a Gallup survey noted that while 41 percent of Americans pledged to boycott Exxon, only 7 percent actually did so. But, after what surely will go down as one of the great crisis management tests of all time, history will judge that they dropped the ball. Stock analysts will consider management attitudes and responsiveness, and some shareholders will think twice about investing in a company with such a questionable corporate conscience.

If past attitudes and awareness research is any guide, many consumers will go the extra distance to make a choice of other than Exxon at the pump, in home heating products, and elsewhere.

As 1996 drew to a close, a public relations disaster befell Texaco, another giant oil company and an Exxon competitor. A tape recording was released to the press and the public on which voices of Texaco executives were heard not only engaging in blatantly racist conversations, but discussing destroying meeting records and other files that clearly constituted a violation of law. Texaco's CEO took to the company's closed circuit TV system and apologized, removed the executives from their positions, said such conduct will never be tolerated in the company, and released a videotape of his emotional address to the press in time for the nightly news. Texaco lawyers met with representatives of the aggrieved parties and agreed to a monetary settlement of more than $100 million.

Some people called the matter an issue of clean, almost surgically neat, damage control. Some said that the biggest issue around Texaco was not what the executives did, but that they got caught and, behind closed doors, the corporate culture was unlikely to change.

Maybe, but virtually no one challenged that Texaco had done the best, if not the only, thing it could under the circumstances and gave the company and its management high marks for moving swiftly. Over the long term, members of some minorities will probably get in the habit of passing Texaco by, but the general feeling is that the incident will be an expensive footnote in the company's history, with no real major damage.

Perhaps Texaco didn't handle its crisis with the cool, easy grace of Mobil, but the company might have learned a lesson from Exxon's state-of-the-art inept handling of its own situation.

At Exxon the flag still flies, but there's dirt on it and all questions about dirt are referred to the legal department.

The Luxury of Fur... It's Not Like It's a Steak

When did it become a crime to enjoy the finer things in life? The answer to that question is that it didn't become a crime, it only became "politically incorrect."

The nice house, big car, fur coat—symbols of status and success—have each been frequently under fire. The dream of home ownership causes sleepless nights to those who see their once stable property values turn shaky, while real estate taxes soar. Refinancing is a way of life, except when a credit crunch keeps lenders from lending. Big cars are attacked as big polluters, small luxury cars as showy symbols of the conspicuous consumption of the1980s.

But no symbol of success has been attacked with such vengeance as the fur coat. Animal rights activist organizations have formed locally and nationally to demonstrate, lobby, boycott, and even physically attack and vandalize fur salons and their customers.

The Society for the Prevention of Cruelty to Animals (SPCA) long had the field to itself as it monitored and informed the public of animal abuses, particularly in laboratory testing and in the entertainment industry. Companies were scrutinized and censured for harmful treatment of animals.

But other organizations have broadened the field and the issues:

- PETA (People for the Ethical Treatment of Animals), one of the more visible groups, has been credited with changes in the use of animals for laboratory testing in the cosmetics industry. It has also taken a strong position against fur industry trapping practices.
- United Action for Animals claims to have collected hundreds of recent research papers, detailing cruelty to animals in laboratory tests.
- The Humane Society of the United States has mounted a highly aggressive advertising campaign aimed at the fur industry.
- Beauty Without Cruelty—U.S.A. launched a campaign on the theme "crimes of fashion" and convinced dozens of celebrities to lend their names to anti-fur magazine ads. The broad-reaching list included such people as Brigitte Bardot, Alice Walker, Cyndi Lauper, and Sting.
- Trans-Species Unlimited says its aim is not only to protect animals, but to limit "animal exploitation" at every level.

There are others—from Friends of Animals to the Animal Liberation Front—large and small, big city and small town; some well-financed, others strictly volunteer-oriented with hand-lettered signs.

What makes the fur industry unique in a crisis marketing sense is both its evolution and the line-up on both sides.

The fur coat had always been the well-dressed woman's symbol of elegance and luxury until 1960s activists made it a line item on their agenda of things wrong with the world:

War, air and water pollution, capitalism, synthetic fibers, and cruel and inhumane treatment of people and animals.

Furriers had trouble understanding the attack back in the days when it was only criticism from a distance. Fur coats were not only beautiful they were practical, warm, long-wearing. Besides, man has been killing animals for clothing since the beginning of time. People weren't out demonstrating against leather shoes and belts. Why them? Why now?

Sensitivity—the post 1960s legacy?

Vanity more than practicality?

There are a number of "whys." True cruelty to animals and graphically described methods of trapping and killing evoke highly emotional responses. Further, for activists searching for a cause, the very elegance of fur coats and their identification with wealth provided an easy target.

But the uniqueness of this situation is that in other crises, such as the Exxon *Valdez* oil spill, it's usually the press and the public asking angrily "so what have you got to say for yourself?" The fur industry has an army of attackers, not particularly interested in justifications, running aggressive "anti" campaigns, similar to the types of campaigns waged by the religious right.

- The Humane Society's ad headline is "You Should Be Ashamed to Wear Fur."
- The Beauty Without Cruelty—U.S.A. campaign says "Say No to Furs."
- Trans-Species Unlimited propaganda shows pictures of pathetic, helpless animals under the headline "Trapped by Greed."

The lead paragraph in an article in the Effingham, Illinois *Daily News* asked, "Is a woman pond scum if she wears a mink coat? According to the Humane Society of the United States, the answer is a resounding *yes.*"

The fur industry counters with an equally aggressive campaign that is built around "freedom of choice."

This is a mistake. It's the same mistake tobacco companies make in trying to defend their position on cigarette smoking. Of course, in both instances some will argue that the point is legitimate. Maybe so.

It has also proven to be unconvincing for years.

If the anti-fur group is going to base its objection to the product on charges of cruelty, "freedom of choice" is a lame response. Cruelty is never a viable, acceptable "choice."

Another ad, run by the Associated Fur Industries, uses the headline "Today fur. Tomorrow leather. Then wool. Then meat ..."

With all due respect, this variation on the freedom theme wasn't and won't be very effective either. It attempts to discredit the critics, a technique that didn't work when General Motors used it against Ralph Nader and won't work today. People didn't feel better about buying GM's alleged unsafe cars because Mr. Nader's quirks made him seem a bit of an odd fellow. Similarly, if the fur buyer is upset with the industry's practices and its treatment of animals and is reconsidering fur in her or his life, being told to turn a deaf ear to the critics because owning a fur coat is a protected freedom will leave the consumer feeling pretty depressed.

Tom Riley, of the Fur Information Council of America, told *New York* magazine that for several years the fur industry had ignored the activists. "We hoped that if we did not respond, it would become a non-event," he said.

But sales dropped and, reluctantly, the industry launched a multi-million-dollar public relations and advertising campaign aimed at attacking its attackers whom they sought to dismiss as terrorists and wild-eyed radicals.

Steve Gold, head of the advertising agency for Saga, a Scandinavian fur producers' cooperative, told the *Wall Street Journal*, "We didn't want to be combative in our advertising because we felt there was nothing to gain."

So while the Saga ads show both subtlety and style, their message still falls short. The message is that "some people are opposed to a very basic luxury, your freedom of choice."

Occasionally, negative political advertising is successful. That's where the best thing a politician can say about his or her own qualities is that there are so many things wrong with an opponent. While overwhelmingly. people say they against negative political ads, evidence shows they are effective. People don't like them, but they still read them and, apparently, even if they don't believe the messages, negative impressions remain. And if the candidate being attacked fails to dignify the negative ad with a response, it is perceived by some people as either an acknowledgement that the attack is justified or as a sign of weakness by the candidate under attack.

So politicians should respond quickly, firmly, directly, and briefly, before then shifting back to a positive message for himself or herself.

With product or brand attack ads, it is not appropriate to respond.

Sometimes a negative (attack) ad leaves a strong enough impression that the message hits home and is not forgotten, and neither **is** the tactic. Negative advertising is usually used when the advertised product's benefits aren't worth talking about. The best, most memorable, most effective advertising focuses on the benefits of the product to the customer.

One Chicago-area retailer drew upon its sixty years in business and prepared a newsletter that addressed its customers on the subjects of quality products and personal service. It noted too that fur trading is the oldest industry in the New World; that no U.S. law prohibits trade of fur from endangered species; that there are more than 1,200 family-run mink farms in the United States, managed by second and third generation breeders.

A statement prepared for press inquiries elaborated on these points, adding, "Fur is an important natural resource, in part because it is renewable, durable, non-polluting, and warm. Further, some furs, such as raccoon and beaver, are over-populated and pose a need for population control."

Such statements might work as responses to questions. The furrier's ads presented a message of luxury and quality, without defensiveness. Once a message becomes defensive, it indirectly brings attention to an opponent's point-of-view. A message that articulates a product's benefits must be judged on its own value, not on points it doesn't make.

The Fur Information Council of America's position makes four points, two of which are simple and self-serving:

- (". . . take pride in hand-crafted garments of exceptional natural beauty" and

- "believe individuals have the right to make the personal choice to own a fur").

It is, however, the other two points that should have set the tone for their campaign up front, not at the very end. Those points are that:
- U.S. fur retailers and manufacturers support responsible treatment of fur-bearing animals and
- are concerned about conservation and our natural environment.

The rationale for this position is that responsible choice is implied, not used to bludgeon.

Here are some recommendations for the furrier under fire:
- Designate one individual within your organization to speak to the animal rights issue. Different employees offering their various comments and opinions can confuse, cloud, and cause comments to be quoted out of context.
- Examine your position carefully on your industry. That is, if you believe in the two points noted above (responsible treatment of fur-bearing animals and concern for conservation and environment), then make it the basis of your position and distance yourself from those in your industry who feel differently. (If you don't believe it, duck—you're in for a rough time.)
- Raise your visibility. Publish a newsletter and/or write to your customers frequently, stressing:
  - your concern for responsible treatment
  - your concern for conservation and the environment
  - benefits to your customers—personal service, quality, value, etc.
- Advertise positively, not defensively. Stress value and quality.
- Designate a flack-catcher in your organization. This might or might not be your spokesperson. The flack-catcher's job is to:

- Extend and accept invitations to discuss (not debate) fur issues with someone having an opposing point-or-view, most likely a very loud and angry animal rights activist.
- Distance yourself from others in your industry who might not share your beliefs. Don't attack or even criticize, but allow for analogies such as in medicine: some doctors use drug therapy, others use herbs. Neither concedes his or her position, yet both exist and the marketplace will determine which of them will be around for the long haul.
- Support causes from Little League to hospital fundraising and publicize your position. Publicizing is not the same as "showboating." A good citizen of the community is not one people want to attack.
- Put your position and your profession in context. Just as farmers breed animals for food, whether chickens, hogs, or cattle, critics will not focus on the fur breeders or trappers as the villains if the process by which they operate is shown to be humane. Show in brochures and ads how the animals are bred for a purpose but are not tortured or abused along the way, certainly not by a good citizen of the community.

Consider that certain crises come about because some special interest groups will target and attack a particular company or industry and pose a series of "are you still beating your wife" questions. If you believe in your business, its legitimacy and integrity, you can get through the crisis. If, however, you are defensive about your role because you really don't believe in your business, then get another job. To be even more simplistic, the Exxon *Valdez* situation could have been contained and less harmful to the company had Exxon acknowledged the problem quickly and sought to make swift restitution. A furrier, however, who hears the charges of the animal rights activists and shrugs at their charges of cruelty cannot expect to find a very supportive constituency. Cruelty and indifference are not marketable commodities.

This is not to suggest that a glib, positive campaign will right any wrong, but if you believe your position is reasonable—and it really is reasonable—you'll be able to get a hearing, and how persuasive a case you make is up to you.

Don't exceed credibility. You're not going to convince people that animals like dying to become coats any more than you'll convince people cattle like dying to become steaks or fish like . . . well, you get the idea. But within the culture in which we live, there are certain acceptable products, fabrics, and foods, and how they come into being can be accepted as reasonable. Concerned, caring, responsible, ethical, and humane are adjectives to describe the characteristics of the marketer and company people want to like, respect, or, at least, have no desire to harm.

If you don't really believe that what you do is proper, following the recommendations outlined here will be only a cosmetic coating and will likely not be very effective for very long. If you believe you are doing the right things in the right way, don't say so, show it, and your constituency will acknowledge it.

Images, Passion, Controversy, Social and Moral Objections . . . All for Only About $6 a Pack

This is a case that should make everyone sit up straight and embrace the idea of crisis marketing or reach for the blood pressure medication. Few subjects cause people in the United States to choose sides immediately and cause passions to rise as much as the subject of smoking. Few industries have been at the center of controversy and crisis as long as the tobacco industry. Each new year, each session of the U.S. Congress, tobacco company executives and advocates on both sides step up and ask, "Will this be the one?"

Sometimes the very idea of American marketers planning and implementing programs while their companies and entire industry are under fire seems outrageous. Yet, virtually each year new brands are introduced, brand extensions proliferate, critics howl, and statistics suggest that after years of health warnings and intensive campaigning to turn people away from tobacco, smoking remains as a significant fact-of-life, especially among the younger generation. And smoking remains popular—and still socially acceptable—in many parts of the world.

Further, after a prolonged period during which both cigar smoking and pipe smoking, considered even more offensive because of emitting a stronger aroma, were banned from those public places that still allowed cigarette smoking, cigar smoking enjoyed a resurgence in popularity to the point of being considered fashionable. Cigar magazines, newsletters, and even private clubs catering to cigar aficionados are across the United States. Major celebrities—both men and women—in sports and entertainment, as well as business leaders, actually seemed to not only enjoy a good cigar, but enjoy being photographed and identified as such. Many delighted in appearing on the cover of an elegantly designed magazine aimed at cigar smokers. Top Hollywood stars pose willingly for posters and ads smoking cigars.

Did this mean the situation had drifted back to normal? Was it okay to smoke again? Were we all once again friends?

Hardly.

Despite such episodes of somewhat detached trendiness, the pressure overall continues to mount. What was once a symbol of sophistication among cultured men and women and rugged machismo among the adventurous outdoor types has mightily fallen from favor with the masses and the media. Critics pressed to make the words *smoking* and *death* synonymous. Ad agencies and tobacco company executives are asked regularly how anyone could market cigarettes with a clear conscience in today's enlightened market environment?

The general consensus is that if something goes wrong—a mistake, even a gross miscalculation—a corporation might respond in any number of ways, regroup, and reenter the marketplace with all corrections and safety mechanisms in place and the public will forgive, forget, and move on.

In this visually rich magazine cover, everyone loses. The tobacco industry—and cigars in particular— are portrayed in this magazine with an "in-your-face" attitude that will not help the cause of either in the long run. That a celebrity must be photographed holding a cigar on every issue's cover is overkill. Some subtlety here might have helped both the subject and the cover celebrity to be taken more seriously.

But how does one take a product to market or respond to critics when it has been banned from public and private places—even, In some cases from entire cities or states—and when the entire medical community has called it a leading cause of more than one form of cancer and a list of other diseases, when activists have publicly decried it and called its marketers "merchants of death," and when politicians from the capitals to the tiniest hamlets have seized the issue as a seemingly sure ticket to reelection?

The answer is that responding to such a challenge makes the question, "are you still beating your wife" seem easy to answer in comparison.

Many of the previous tactics discussed in other cases have been tried by the tobacco industry with very little impact, much less success. The product itself, tobacco, is at the very center of the storm. Certainly this represents an enormous cultural shift. For decades in classic sophisticated motion pictures major stars, from Cary Grant, Katharine Hepburn, William Powell, Myrna Loy, Bette Davis, and Humphrey Bogart, James Dean, Sharon Stone, and Al Pacino, among others, would never attempt the most casual repartee, let alone a seduction, without first a long soulful draw on a cigarette.

In addition, governments have subsidized tobacco farmers for years and support from the industry seemed virtually a requirement for one seeking public office. And the taxes on tobacco products account for the single largest portion of their purchase price.

As health concerns grow, the tobacco industry follows the historic corporate script of first dismissing the questions, studies, and reports as inconclusive, attacking their attackers, and, finally, falling back on the patriotic stance that smoking was a "freedom" and, as such, protected by the blood of our forefathers. Millions of dollars were spent on this approach. Perhaps *wasted* is a better word.

An R. J. Reynolds Tobacco Company ad some years ago was even somewhat embarrassing to read for its patronizing approach to the controversy. In a vertically split page that professed to offer a "debate" on issues, offering smokers' views in one column, non-smokers in the other, both sides' arguments seemed thin, staged, and unworthy of a junior high school debate team. The very not-so-subtle suggestion was that there are two sides to the issue and if each side would just respect the other's position and leave each other alone, the world would be a better place.

Smokers waved it off, annoyed at the arrogance, insulting behavior, and "holier than thou" attitudes of the anti-smokers. Non-smokers felt very much the same way and for the same reasons.

What was then called the Philip Morris Companies took the freedom issue a step further In America by sponsoring a very heavily advertised historic and powerful five-state tour of The National Archives celebration of the 200th anniversary of The Bill of Rights. Its presentation was described as "an extraordinary exhibition that will capture their eyes, their ears and, most of all, their hearts. They'll be enveloped by history, transported into the present, and reenter the world with a new appreciation of our freedoms."

And then, presumably, they'll want to kick back and light up.

The very presence of the Philip Morris logo told people what specific freedoms were being called into question.

Another Philip Morris ad pictured New York City Ballet principal dancer Valennna Kozlova and the headline quote, "Defection was difficult. Not being free was worse." The accompanying text was a very moving commentary on freedom, very moving and, critics suggested, very transparent.

The public responded with a vote of agreement on the importance of freedom, but asked what does all that have to do with the studies showing that smoking causes cancer, birth defects, and any number of other difficulties?

The tobacco companies' position, however, was that what studies show about anything should be a matter of information or education, but ultimately a medical school study should not override the U.S. Constitution by requesting or demanding a ban on products or a limitation of an individual's freedom to use such products.

Smokers continue smoking and voicing their annoyance at not being able to smoke in most restaurants, airports, and public buildings.

Non-smokers bristle and continue to resent smokers, the tobacco companies, their ad agencies, and whatever media carries their ads. One faction held that a public display of rudeness was socially acceptable if directed at someone smoking.

R. J. Reynolds Tobacco became RJR Nabisco and through this consolidation with the giant food company, it has become an even bigger giant, thus slightly taking the edge off the tobacco company target, before spinning off to be separate again.

The Philip Morris Companies, too, became a more diversified conglomerate, adding such units as Kraft Foods and Miller Brewing, but continued to lead the public charge in defense of its products. In or around 1985, *Philip Morris Magazine* made its debut. This slick, colorful quarterly was distributed by mail, compliments of Philip Morris U.S.A. Early issues took the advertorial a step, or perhaps light years, ahead by publishing articles for and about smokers, separated by ads for the company's various brands. The articles were first-rate. Writing, graphics, and printing were all comparable to the best newsweekly. The magazine didn't change non-smokers' attitudes, but clearly didn't intend to. With surveys, free offers, and articles aimed at the smoker, the publication's goal was clearly to help stabilize the market in which the company was so heavily invested. Smokers were being attacked and they were hating it. This magazine was telling them they were okay, they were among friends— tens of millions of other smokers all over the world—and not to be intimidated.

Suggestions were offered as to which members of Congress one should write and what should be written, usually regarding the rights of the tens of millions of voting, tax-paying smokers.

With time, the magazine became much more subtle in its approach, though it never hid nor apologized for its position. Its very name—*Philip Morris Magazine*—was hardly a sign of the company's desire to conceal its presence or its perceived importance,

Later issues featured numerous stories and articles far from the subject of smoking, articles such as "The Six Meanest Linebackers in the NFL," by Dan Dierdorf of ABC-TV's *Monday Night Football,*

The creative approach is patronizing, as is the ad copy itself. The company might have done better had it skipped the ad altogether and offered a variation of the message in a direct mail letter to parents (released to the press). The particular issue, to benefit the advertiser, needs *less* visibility, not more.

and "Rock Star" about Lynn Hill, the world's number-one rock climber. And the publisher was no longer the magazine's only advertiser. While far from self-supporting, a typical issue might carry ads from clothing manufacturers and watchmakers in addition to the ads **for** various PM cigarette brands and other products under the corporate umbrella.

But with all the editorial and artistic slickness promised in the cover's "The Best of America" legend, it was the magazine's six-or-so-page Forum section toward the back of the book where the true purpose of the publication took center stage. Under such headings as "perspectives," "viewpoints," "in my opinion," and "smoke signals," the magazine published letters from readers and columns from contributors— including the company's own chairman.

"We acknowledge that there is a statistical association between cigarette smoking and some human diseases. Most scientists would agree, however, that statistical association does not prove causation," the chairman wrote.

While this argument had been made before and consistently failed to impress critics, the company's chairman went further: "Our view on causation, however, does not lessen our concern that risk factors have been recognized. Nor does it lessen our commitment to fund independent scientific research designed to help clarify the causes of human disease. We want our customers to be aware of the risk factors involved, and we believe they are."

This, of course, while, as the lawyers like to say, without admitting or denying the charges, should have been a little further toward the front of the magazine than page 39—like, perhaps on page *one*—"chairman's page." Yet, the publishers placed it where they did so the magazine would hold reader interest with its features and stories before taking to the soapbox.

A letter from a reader in California told that a traveling companion's smoking hadn't bothered him at all, yet how offended he was that another individual seemed to go out of her way to cause a scene in attempting to embarrass the smoker. Another reader, from New York, was offended as a frequent flyer by the ban on smoking during domestic flights. A woman from Fort Myers, Florida, closed her letter to the magazine with "I am fed up with the anti-smoking campaign: It is unfair and discriminates against smokers."

Philip Morris, of course, must modestly beam that a reader would say what they themselves would like to say, but have chosen not to, lest it be viewed as combative and widen the gulf between factions.

Quite wisely, Philip Morris positioned its name and products in a wider universe than just a carton of cigarettes, with diversified brands, funding of PBS television shows, and sponsorships such as the twelve "Virginia Slims" tennis tournaments. Merchandise catalogs appeared, offering entire lines of both Camel and "Joe Camel" merchandise, from jackets to lighters, coffee mugs, beach towels, and more. The legendary Marlboro Man was joined by the Marlboro Adventure Team, which was anyone who bought the cigarettes, saved the coupons, and ordered catalog merchandise that was high-quality sports, camping, and gaming accessories. On the more elegant side, the Benson & Hedges Home Collection Catalog offered tasteful accessories and furnishings that would blend nicely into homes with names like Astor or Rockefeller on the mailbox. The idea was, of course, to identify the name of the cigarette brand with fun, elegant, or interesting items of quality that had nothing to do with the cigarettes themselves. Extend the brand image beyond the cigarette or the pack into the customer's life in a tasteful, totally inoffensive way. Smokers loved the stuff; non-smokers gasped at someone out jogging in T-shirt and running shorts bearing the Camel logo. It is reasonable to say that the already angry critics remained so, while smokers or disinterested parties enjoyed what they considered quality products at value prices.

The Tobacco Institute, the industry trade group, ran ads in major U.S. newspapers, including the *New York Times* and *USA Today,* with headlines reading, "What's the tobacco industry doing to discourage youth smoking?" The ad copy answered the question, and the institute further said its thirteen member companies had agreed not to offer product sampling on public streets and sidewalks and would not pay for product placements in films.

This announcement was attacked by anti-smoking groups and

legislators as a public relations gesture and there may be some legitimacy to the charge. But why is that necessarily a bad thing? The very essence of public relations requires that one spread the news about good things done. A problem with the message is that it subtly admits wrongdoing.

Consider that one of the most important components of a crisis marketing plan is that it should be positive without being defensive. To say you are going to stop paying to have your product placed in films—a practice common in film production since the 1960s—is acknowledging your product has characteristics about which you yourself are uncomfortable. In issuing this announcement, the industry offered its critics yet another opportunity to attack them in public. If they wanted to discontinue the "pay for placement" policy, to have done it without fanfare would have been wiser. At some point it would have been noted publicly and the industry could take a bow. Doing it as they did, in hopes of getting credit for the move, backfired.

Likewise, when the R. J. Reynolds Company, which had intended to market Uptown, a cigarette brand aimed at African Americans, found its marketing plan made public, it back-peddled in embarrassment and stalled the product launch.

Why?

Eve and Virginia Slims were both marketed specifically to women who, the companies believed, would buy a cigarette created just for them. If a manufacturer is going to go to the trouble to ask if African Americans have specific taste preferences in a cigarette, how is that any different than targeting any other product, such as targeting extra spicy foods to ethnic audiences with a historic preference for such products? It was different because the industry was in a defensive posture and prepared to retreat at the first shot fired.

In an interview with the *New York Times,* the company defended its position, but that then became part of the problem: they were being defensive, instead of (again, to praise the Mobil Oil approach) taking a direct stand that showed a strong belief in the legitimacy of its position, which was to tell its story without apology. When critics charged that a brand aimed at black people was an attempt by the tobacco company to exploit inner-city black consumers, the company panicked. Since any number of companies had been marketing specialized as well as mainstream products to African Americans for years, Reynolds might have simply told critics under such circumstances to grow up.

The tricky question today is how can the tobacco industry, charged with causing any number of diseases, continue to market its products in such a climate? Perhaps, like the blacksmith and door-to-door salesman, tobacco is a product that no longer fits into modern life. Perhaps.

Many people believe the pendulum will swing the other way and, like the aggressive anti-fur groups, the anti-smoking faction will annoy enough people, make their case enough times, picket and demonstrate and sue to garner so much attention that it will cause the public to say "Enough already!"

The editor of *Cigar Aficionado* magazine continues to stress, "Smokers have rights too." The argument is not likely to sway people who've given the issue a lot of thought, but when the lofty case is made for the type of society people wish to have, individual freedom always tends to come out high on the list.

On the issue of the rise in teen smoking, the companies are in a tough spot. On one side is the simple reality that teenagers have experimented or tried smoking as part of the coming-of-age ritual probably since the concept of high school was introduced—or before. But, in an effort to do something before the government did something, virtually all of the tobacco companies ran ads announcing they were against underage persons smoking. The Philip Morris ad showed a headline apparently written in crayon in a child's scrawl: Kids should not smoke. It's doubtful that much of a dramatic impression was made. R. J, Reynolds offered a costly package of brochures and other literature to parents who wanted help in discouraging their children from smoking. It was actually a very well-done package, graphically, editorially, and conceptually, and or high production value. The cover letter urging parents to write to their congressmen, senators, and the Food and

Drug Administration, urging that federal bureaucrats not interfere further in the rights of smokers was probably not the smartest move strategically.

In reality, if the government is likely to ban tobacco products, as liquor was banned in the 1920s, the industry better have a lot of cookies and pies to fall back on. A product in such wide and accepted usage for so long will simply find an alternative delivery system. But since it is unlikely that such a ban will occur in the foreseeable future, the U.S. government at this time apparently believing that smoking should remain an optional legal vice and governments elsewhere showing little concern as smoking increases generally in other countries, here are some suggestions.

"Joe Camel has left the building..." and these examples of how a tobacco company (Reynolds) is trying to win public approval for its stand on "Youth Smoking" are bright, commendable, expensive, and not very believable. The company might have done better had it not tried to make people believe it would really act against its own self-interests.

Talk to your public.

While the Philip Morris magazine had the look and feel of a quality publication in its own right, it was clearly a thinly disguised propaganda vehicle, with an emphasis on the word *thinly*. Pro-freedom/pro-smoker articles and editorials in the back of the magazine reinforce this perception. Move these articles up from—to page one—and identify that "This is a magazine created with people who smoke in mind. They're our customers and we appreciate their business and their support." Additionally, designate articulate, well-informed spokespersons. These people will come to be regarded as "The Faces of the Tobacco Industry." They should not, therefore, resemble the Grim Reaper. The anti-smoking groups use former cigarette-smoking celebrities and a former **U.S.** surgeon general as spokespeople. The tobacco industry has anonymous ad agency copywriters writing what appear to be editorials, yet are either unsigned or over a corporate signature.

Positioning a friendly individual against a huge corporation works against the corporation. Designate individuals to speak, whether they are corporate officers or professional spokespeople. They don't even have to be smokers to articulate that adult pleasures should be an option to adults, as long as governments declare them to be legal.

Personalize your story.

If you believe in the persuasiveness of your argument, use advertorials. The shortcoming of most tobacco company ads is that they are heavy on editorial copy that either takes an overly defensive or an overly patronizing tone. Smoking is not a matter of patriotism, so wrapping a cigarette in the Bill of Rights probably won't get you very far. To succeed, one must believe in the correctness of one's position.

An interesting approach was used for several years by the Carlton cigarette brand. In magazine ads and billboards, the company, without any graphics at all, just carried the line, "If you're going to smoke, please smoke Carlton," and listed the brand's low nicotine content. While at first glance the line seems embarrassingly light and almost as if the company is begging the consumer to buy the product, a second reading suggests a sensitivity to the smokers' desire to smoke and a plea to opt for the "least harmful" brand—almost like a support system for the guilt-ridden smoker. This approach was interesting, but became so familiar in its simplicity and repetition as to go unnoticed after a time.

Benson & Hedges enjoyed fine sales in the 1980s with curious yuppie-like photoplays—print ads using photos without captions: a shirtless man in pajama bottoms passing through a room where a group of clearly "upscale" people were enjoying a wonderful lunch, brunch, or dinner; a very warm scene of a group of thirty-something women enjoying a reunion or other kind of "bonding" experience over a great meal. These campaigns gained considerable attention in major media. (The TV show *Entertainment Tonight* posed the question, "Who is the pajama man?" and built a good-natured feature piece around the ad, generating a wealth of free publicity.) No one raised the issue during this episode of the dangers of cigarette smoking. The Marlboro Man continued to be the strong, silent type, merely tending to his outdoor, deep-woods, open-range chores and lifestyle, and enjoying a good, manly smoke when he wanted one (despite the fact that the gentleman who appeared in the ads contracted lung cancer and, for a time, spoke out against the product that made him a wealthy advertising icon).

Merit, another Philip Morris product, advertised a pack of its cigarettes under the headline "We don't show people smoking in our ads." Copy below the headline read "Because we figure smokers already know how. Heck, we're not talking rocket science here. So, we'll get right to the point: flavor." This very direct, somewhat tongue-in-cheek approach spoke to adults, without macho or trendy imagery.

This is all to say that if people choose to smoke cigarettes, cigarette advertising, when done well, still works. One cannot sell a brand in a crowded field without brand visibility. Brands through their advertising and, to a limited degree, their packaging are reflective of lifestyle: manly, feminine, successful. The line

"You've come a long way, baby," became as much a slogan of the feminist movement as it was for Virginia Slims cigarettes—for more than 20 years.

Put your product in a larger context.

Don't let your critics position your product for you. The Carl-ton slogan, "If you're going to smoke, please smoke Carlton," shows that smoking is a part of what some people have chosen to do, but it's not *all* that they do. This gets tricky. Often smoking is compared—and paired—with drinking. Fairly thin arguments are offered about how both might be bad, but can't be that bad or they would be illegal. This is a losing argument that no marketer should ever expect to win. Why would anyone take a perceived negative, couple it with another perceived negative and believe that the net result would be positive? Remember that pointing up the negative points of your product is something that your critics do. You should anticipate it, but volunteering negative information is not your responsibility as a marketer. The health risk has been mandated by law to be identified on packaging and in ads. But don't go further than you have to based on supposition and possibilities. That is, warn about things you know, not about things that might be.

Red meat might contribute to any number of health problems. Sugar, we are told, adds weight, causes dental problems, promotes hyperactivity in children, and any number of other difficulties. Dairy products, high in fat, reportedly promote heart disease. Yet no one has called for warnings on labels or in ads. Lack of exercise poses a health problem. So does too much exercise. Broccoli, a high-fiber food, may help prevent cancer. Millions of people jumped on the bandwagon, believing that a few pounds of oat bran might help reduce cholesterol, thus lessening the risk of a heart attack. Then, again, maybe not. A noted heart specialist suggested the best thing—maybe the only good thing—about "the oat bran craze" was that it kept people from eating eggs for breakfast. The dairy industry groaned their disagreement at the inference. Take critics' attacks seriously, but recognize—and point out—that virtually every industry has its critics who would like to see it regulated out of business.

In 1964, humorist Max Shulman wrote a novel called *Anyone Got a Match?* The premise of the book was a cigarette company's defending itself against "health-scare nuts" by launching "a sensationally vigorous offensive against anything humanly ingestible, mainly food." Shulman detailed the use of additives in such products as cake mixes, vitamin capsules, peanut butter, and any number of other foods—some of the same chemical additives that are, basically, paint remover. He wrote of laboratory mice developing bladder cancer from a dye used to color butter and margarine and certified by the FDA. And skin cancers caused by using various chemicals and dyes in various foods . . . Well, you get the idea. Shulman's book was fiction, but his data was fact-based. Certainly the FDA and the food industry have made advances since 1964? Or have they?

In 1994 Christopher Buckley similarly satirized the subject in a bestselling book, which became a successful 2006 Hollywood film, called *Thank You for Smoking.*

If Joe Camel can't appear on TV, the company will settle instead for appearing everywhere else. The merchandising is clever and entertaining. It has given critics more bullets to fire back at the company, but already having chosen not to hide, promoting the character and merchandise seemed like a better idea than promoting the product or smoking. A 1997 controversy over the character will turn these into collectors' items.

Nutritionists and dieticians continue to express outrage at the amounts of fats, sugar, chemicals, and preservatives in the most popular foods on the American dinner table. In the opinion of many health-care professionals, the "four basic food groups"—particularly the meat and dairy components—might well be doing more harm than good.

In any event, it is not advocated here that the tobacco industry should respond to its critics by attacking the food industries or suggesting that "eating is as bad as smoking." It is, however, suggested that smoking as a health risk be shown in context. A number of smokers are athletes and successful singing stars. That doesn't make smoking healthy or even okay, but it shows that smokers are people with lives and jobs. Dismissing them as evil, unclean, or unsavory is simply not appropriate.

Statesmen smoke. And writers. Are they proud of it? Probably not. Do they flaunt this fact? No. They also don't focus on it and neither should the tobacco companies.

Consider redefining your positioning.

This, more than anything else, represents a huge departure from the way in which the industry has historically sold its products. Why should they reposition when they are making mega-millions, even in bad years? Because the tobacco industry is under attack, defensive, facing huge legal and public relations challenges, and because it cares about these things.

Cigarette companies can no longer get away with, much less thrive on, campaigns that position smoking as a glamorous, sophisticated, pleasurable part of the best lifestyles. Yes, sales are up internationally and, yes, again, the number of women and young people smoking is on the increase. Proportionately, so are the problems.

Smoking might be, then, repositioned as an exclusively adult pleasure, expensive and maybe risky, but an option of a certain lifestyle.

Fast cars are expensive and dangerous. Driving any car fast is dangerous. While there are speed limits, there are designated places where people who so choose can drive fast. Are such people crazy? Some think so, but others acknowledge that the personal choice for excitement and pleasure is an option not to be denied. The same types of arguments can be made for a virtually endless list of things from skydiving, hot-air ballooning, deep sea fishing, prize-fighting, mountain climbing, nightclubbing, bullfighting, white-water rafting, and more.

Dangerous, risky under the best conditions, pleasurable, and sometimes expensive—the difference is that, over the years, the tobacco companies have positioned their product for the masses—for everyone. In current market climates, few things are appropriate for everyone. Times have changed.

If the concept of cigarette smoking were being introduced today, it would be only after endless amounts of research and study and finely targeted to a specific demographic segment. From there, it might have an opportunity to build, but a serious marketer would position the product carefully and target a segment. Currently, by saying only that they do not encourage or intentionally entice children to smoke, the industry offers only the most half-hearted suggestion that they don't believe their products are for everyone. Everyone doesn't drink champagne or cola. Not everyone watches baseball or listens to opera. In the face of the public outcry that often borders on panic, just to say that smoking is not for everyone is an absurdly inadequate response.

Critics often attack at the most vulnerable points. Camel Cigarettes has been around for decades and enjoys a huge market share with more than a half-dozen brand extensions (regulars, filters, light, extra light, menthol, etc.), but the greatest amount of criticism of the product is for its use **of** "Joe" the cartoon Camel in scenes from racing cars to nightclubs. The charge is that the campaign is aimed at enticing children to smoke. The company denies this, noting it has used the character in ads for years—the most recent version of the campaign rolled out in 1987 and appeared to be still going strong nearly ten years later. Camel claims that it's a fun-loving campaign, that smoking is one of life's pleasures. The critics don't believe them. In simple fact, people who are predisposed against a product or brand will rather easily accept any argument char validates their position, regardless of its validity.

Should Camel cigarettes drop the "Joe Camel" cartoon character from its ads and merchandising?

No. Despite having said it would in 1997, the character is likely to reappear in foreign usage and in promotional collectibles. While advertisers should be responsive to claims that their ads are obscene or offensive, ads should not be pulled because they are entertaining or memorable. Camel should do the best marketing of its product that it can within the limitations set down for tobacco companies by regulators and legislators. Advertising might indeed (if it's doing what it's supposed to do) influence the selection of a brand. But a cartoon character in an ad will not make a non-smoker smoke any more than a singing, dancing, juggling chicken—cartoon or otherwise—will make someone buy chicken who doesn't like chicken.

On a more serious level, the health issues, with their legal ramifications, must be taken more seriously than matters of cartoon figures in ads. If the result of virtually every study, by virtually every credible source, says your product unequivocally is a killer in no uncertain terms, then your problem, quite simply, is more than a marketing problem. If book after book and numerous magazine articles and TV news shows feature former employees who suggest a conspiracy to withhold information of life-and-death significance, those charges must be addressed quickly and directly. The accusers must be either taken to court for lying or recognized by the companies as heroes for bringing an issue to public attention so the situation can be made right.

Employees, whether chairman of the board or mailroom clerk, cannot be protected if that person has in any way put the company or its customers at risk.

And what if the charges that the product is harmful are true?

Stanton Glantz, a professor of medicine at the University of California at San Francisco, has been an anti-smoking activist for more than twenty years, writing and speaking extensively about cigarette smoking. In a 1996 book, *The Cigarette Papers,* he charges "thirty years ago the tobacco industry knew that nicotine was an addictive substance and that it caused cancer." A spokesman for the Tobacco Institute counters that the professor "is a key player in the movement to manufacture scare tactics by health activists." Again, if the charge is true, those people charged with knowing should be held accountable. If it is not, the company needs to make that clear, though, admittedly, it is somewhat difficult to prove what exactly someone truly didn't know thirty years ago.

In a worst-case situation, the government would have to make a ruling that would punish tobacco companies by either restricting or banning the sale of products. In 1996, the president moved to curtail cigarette marketing dramatically and declare tobacco an addictive substance. Whether or how long such restrictions realistically will last, given America's experience with both Prohibition and ongoing sale and use of addictive substances, is hard to guess. Once a subject becomes the focus of a political campaign it tends to take on a life of its own, certainly outside of the marketing area. For the short-term, the tobacco company marketers need to represent themselves as having provided a product that has been not only, as the old argument held, what the public wanted, but one that was legal, highly regulated, and heavily taxed.

Offer without defensiveness or equivocation that:

- Smoking is for adults only.
- Some people may be offended by others smoking in their presence. Some might not.
- Like a lot of things in life that bring you pleasure, smoking is not without risk.
- As with many other adult pleasures, smoking can be considered a social and cultural choice.

There is little doubt that the bashing will continue into the foreseeable future.

Some members of the public will maintain that smoking kills. Period. And no defense will suffice. Politicians who took campaign contributions from tobacco growers for years will cut and run, proclaiming their shock and dismay that some people are experiencing negative effects from smoking, if that's the way the political wind is blowing at the time.

Don't ignore those voices, answer them—directly and calmly. But do more than just talk to them. Go beyond the controversy and sell the quality of your product.

For the person who says the surgeon general's reports seem pretty conclusive: if, indeed, he or she contends flatly that "smoking causes lung cancer, heart disease, emphysema, and may complicate pregnancy"—if cigarettes are absolutely that dangerous, why are they even still being manufactured and sold? Why aren't they off the market completely instead of merely subjected to restrictions on cigarette advertising?

That's a good question. And not one the marketing department should be called upon to answer. Indeed, a trap many marketers fall into is in trying to argue both sides of an issue. Believe in the integrity of your side and argue only that.

The best guess is that, despite that apparently definitive wording of the package warning, there are conflicting opinions that still warrant consideration. Some people will continue to want, enjoy, and support the product. Others, in the manner of the times, will fight to limit its availability . . . and in that lies the challenge to the marketer.

By 1997, the debate had escalated again. Through a series of lawsuits filed against tobacco companies by various state attorneys general, seemingly ambitious politicians had laid claim to the issue of making cigarette producers pay for the medical care of people who claim smoking had ruined their health. In a bizarre move, a group of tobacco company executives worked out a "settlement," according to which the tobacco companies would stop advertising, discourage kids from smoking, make the warning on cigarette packs larger, and on and on. Whether or not the courts or the Congress of the United States will uphold and enforce such an agreement remains to be seen. Whether the next crop of tobacco company lawyers will support or reverse the companies' legal position, just as courts are often reversing the decisions of other courts, remains to be seen. Companies that have made billions of dollars by catering to public tastes have no historic precedent for either agreeing to stop or for stopping. An increasingly litigious society will not stop pursuing opportunities for restitution or personal gain because someone else has signed an agreement. And individuals—from gun owners to nudists to minorities to seniors—will fight back in large numbers if they believe their freedoms are being curtailed, whether their position is debatable or not. Court challenges, regardless of which side one takes, will be a fact of life for many years to come. So will smoking. The role of the marketer will not disappear, but it will change as the product is repositioned.

In 1998 the "Master Settlement Agreement" between major tobacco companies and attorneys general from 46 states is signed in an effort to dispose of the myriad of lawsuits brought against the companies by smokers and/or their families.

As tobacco companies struggle—creatively and otherwise—to respond to changes in the marketing landscape for products, some notable shifts and changes have occurred at the industry's two largest companies.

Philip Morris acquired Miller Brewing Co. in 1970 and General Foods in 1985. In 1988, it acquired Kraft and combined it with General Foods a year later, creating the largest food company in the United States. Philip Morris acquired Nabisco Holdings and integrated it into Kraft Foods in 2000. In 2001, it conducted an initial public offering of Kraft Foods shares, retaining an 89 percent stake in the food company. In 2003 Miller Brewing merged with South African Breweries to form SABMiller, with Philip Morris retaining a minority interest in the company. In 2003 the Philip Morris Companies Inc. changed its name to Altria Group, Inc. It remains one of the largest tobacco companies in the world. Altria spins off its Kraft subsidiary as a separate company in March.

R. J. Reynolds Tobacco Company (RJR), founded in 1874, is the second-largest tobacco company in the U.S. (behind Altria Group). RJR is an indirect wholly owned subsidiary of Reynolds American Inc. Both companies have been at the eye of the storm for decades.

In 2002 RJR was fined $15 million for distributing free cigarettes at events attended by children, and was fined $20 million for breaking a 1998 agreement between tobacco companies and 46 states, which restricts targeting youth in its tobacco advertisements. In October 2002, the European Community accused R. J. Reynolds of selling black market cigarettes to drug traffickers and mobsters from Italy, Russia, Colombia and the Balkans. Clearly, the preceding two sentences could be the subject of a Crisis book by themselves. This section, however has limited to subject to the issue of responding to critics of smoking.

[Author's note: Much of the material in the foregoing section was created in 1991 for the first edition of this work, and was modified for a second edition, published in 1997. While essentially constructed around applicable crisis management principles and techniques that remain viable, additional edits were necessary for this edition.]

You Think You've Got a Headache? Johnson & Johnson Knows Just How You Feel

Companies large and small, young and old agree: no one is immune. Regardless of the lengths to which one might go to ensure quality control at all levels, a sick-minded person, out to tamper with a product and inject it with a dangerous substance, has the company constantly at risk.

In 1991, the media reported that several people had become ill after taking what were claimed to have been poisoned Sudafed cold tablets. The victims' family members were interviewed and the reporter shook his head sadly. So did viewers. About one minute into the next news story, the matter pretty much seemed to have been forgotten.

Huh?

A poisoning of innocent consumers involving one of America's largest-selling cold medications and there's no stop-the-presses cry for vengeance upon the manufacturer... and, by the way, millions of dollars of settlement money?

No. Instead, there's a consumer public all but casually dismissing the matter as the work of "some nut out there."

Under normal circumstances the lawyers would have shouted that the pharmaceutical company should have protected consumers. It was their responsibility. But these weren't normal circumstances. Normal circumstances sort of don't exist anymore.

The pharmaceutical company knew what it had to do to contain the matter and how to do it. The textbook on the handling of such situations was written in 1982 by Johnson & Johnson, following what has come to be called simply *the Tylenol crisis*. What it was in actuality was perhaps the most astute and competent handling of a major consumer problem in the history of the American corporation.

For years people have become increasingly familiar with the phrase "America has become a litigious society." There is an abundance of lawyers, ready to sue for virtually any reason. No group is more sensitized to this premise than corporate America. The size of the legal department has grown proportionate to the number of complaints and threats of legal action. Where once the preoccupation was only with marketing a good product and serving the consumer, all corporations in the country today devote considerable energy to "making sure we don't get sued."

Once getting a bad meal in a restaurant meant only that a person would not eat there again. By current standards, people calculate how many millions that bad meal might be worth to them in a suit for pain and suffering—and perhaps embarrassment in the presence of dining companions.

Insurance rates soar.

Disclaimers on packaging dominate, often demanding more space than the products' statement of benefits. Why? As a warning for the safety of the consumer? Only partially. The primary reason is to position against lawsuits. The warning, dosage, directions, ingredients, and safety notice on a typical food or household package is so small the best eyesight could not read it easily. The government regulators, of course, realize it. They don't demand that it be read, they demand only that it be there.

In September 1982, following the deaths of seven people in the Chicago area from what appeared to be poisoning, corporate America braced itself. This was no ordinary murderer or serial killer. Circumstances showed all the victims had recently taken the pain-reliever Extra-Strength Tylenol in capsule form. The capsules, authorities said, had been laced with cyanide. As is customary following such reports, a bandwagon effect followed. More reports of illness and death surfaced implicating Tylenol.

That some people were dead was a tragedy. That others would seek to capitalize on the tragedy was the type of response corporations had come to expect. The difference was that this time Tylenol's manufacturer, the pharmaceutical and home products company Johnson & Johnson, a then ninety-six-year-old corporate mainstream giant, behaved in a decidedly *un*-mainstream way.

Rather than present a stance of tight-lipped defensiveness, Johnson & Johnson was forthright and candid from the first accounts of the tragedy. Cooperative with authorities and accessible to the media, the company fielded thousands of calls and inquiries. Their damage control plan included:

- expression of compassion and sympathy for those affected
- an immediate recall of the entire lot—some 93,000 units— from which the tainted bottles were said to have originated
- laboratory tests to assure that the product was not tampered with at the factory, but in fact after it left John-son & Johnson's McNeil Laboratories
- suspension of all product advertising while the story was in the news
- an offer of a $100,000 reward for information leading to the arrest and conviction of the person or persons who tampered with the product
- warnings issued to doctors and hospitals
- a full national recall of all Tylenol brand capsules in the week that followed the tragedy
- serving public notice that it would exchange any outstanding packages of Tylenol capsules for tablet versions of the brand's product

- public appearances on major television programs, including the hard-hitting 60 *Minutes* TV news magazine, to respond to questions in an attempt to maintain and restore brand confidence
- a further appearance on the highly-watched nationally syndicated Phil Donohue show with Johnson & Johnson's chairman, James E. Burke, answering questions from viewers and members of the studio audience for a full hour
- a reintroduction of Extra-Strength Tylenol capsules in triple seal, tamper-resistant packaging, setting a new standard for such types of consumer product

The larger a company is, the more attractive a target it presents to those individuals who might find opportunities to damage it.

In the book *We're So Big and Powerful Nothing Bad Can Happen to Us*, lan Mitroff and Thierry Pauchant argue that:

> The Tylenol case is enough to dispel the notion that only poorly managed companies have major crises. Johnson & Johnson . . . has been regarded for years as an enlightened, ethical, well-managed and respected company. Unfortunately, this did not prevent them from experiencing a major crisis.
>
> . . . J&J rightly and legitimately has been touted as a corporate role model for how to deal with a major crisis.
>
> . . . CEO James Burke did not dodge the press, react with anger or stonewall the problem. [The company] even kept a faithful log of press inquiries so [they] could get back with information when they had it. It responded quickly and effectively to the general . . . public and this restored confidence both in it as a company and in Tylenol as a product.

Estimates show that the product recall alone cost the company nearly $100 million—an amount it accepted with a stiff upper lip.

To its credit, Johnson & Johnson didn't expend all of its energy congratulating itself on its handling of the situation, as some four years later tragedy struck again. In New York a woman died and it was said that poisoned Extra-Strength Tylenol capsules were involved. The company removed the product from the market permanently and replaced it with caplets, capsule-shaped tablets, offering anyone having the capsules a full refund or replacement product. An astonishing 95 percent opted for the exchange rather than money, an amazing vote of confidence for the company. The public believed overwhelmingly that Johnson & Johnson had been as much victimized by the deranged killer as those victims who actually died. This type of popular support for a corporation might well be unprecedented.

Through candor, responsiveness, and sensitivity to its constituents, the company and its brand not only retained its market lead, but won additional respect from its customers, shareholders, and the media. After years of asking consumers to be loyal to the brand, the company showed its sense of loyalty to its customers.

Thomas L. Harris, Managing Partner of Thomas L. Harris & Company cites the case as "the penultimate example of the successful interaction of responsible management action, media relations, and marketing communications."

The company itself offers that they don't believe any special crisis management training might have better prepared them for a situation of this type. Rather, they believe that a good management team, responding as they did, was enough. What that belief failed to acknowledge was years of manufacturing and distributing quality products to consumers and the company's excellent reputation in the marketplace as a good corporate citizen. They had positioned themselves very well, apparently even better than they, themselves, might have thought. Based on years of being a good brand "name," the public wanted to believe Johnson & Johnson was a company of good people doing the right thing. When management responded as openly and broadly as it did, it indeed validated itself in the public mind. Johnson & Johnson's customers believed that their trust was well placed and the goodwill the company had shown was returned in support, loyalty, and consistently increased sales.

Pepsi Shows Quality Under Pressure

Pepsi is a great company with a fine product line. They have, however, for one so clean, had more than their share of rain on their parade.

Always eager to attract a youthful audience, the company signed pop singing star Michael Jackson at the height of his career to appear in a series of commercials for a highly publicized obscene amount of money. Mr. Jackson reported for work on the set and, due to a problem with one of the special effects, his hair caught on fire. Later, of course, he reinvented the entire concept of bad publicity by being arrested and charged with child abuse and, while not ever admitting to the charges, settling out of court for an undisclosed, but rumored to be enormous, amount of money. After a brief marriage to Elvis Presley's daughter, Mr. Jackson announced his nurse was pregnant with his child. They quietly wed. Throughout, Pepsi had no comment—although it has quietly moved to put distance between itself and Michael Jackson.

The company next signed the pop superstar Madonna to appear in its commercials at about the same time religious groups publicly voiced their outrage at what they considered blasphemy and poor taste in her latest music video. Pepsi chose not to extend its association with Madonna.

One of the most bizarre instances of the famous Pepsi can being in the wrong place ended up being an attempt to commit a fraud on the company and backfired in the wrongdoers' faces. Finally, Pepsi had something it wanted to talk about with the news media. It came out well and had itself to credit.

It's human nature to cheer for "the little guy," to hope he pulls off a *surprise upset,* cutting the big guy down to size. That sort of posturing happens a lot when an individual, believing that he or she has been treated badly, goes after a corporate giant.

In most instances when participants are compared to David and Goliath, nobody wants to be Goliath. It's not only that Goliath was the big loser in the story, it has a lot to do with images. David was brave and resourceful, Goliath was mighty, arrogant, and a little slow. So David not only emerges victorious, but makes a fool out of the big guy, many times his size.

There are, of course, exceptions to every story. Johnson & Johnson was a "Goliath"—a huge company, certainly a lot larger in every respect than the disgruntled former employee who was said to be the perpetrator of the Tylenol poisonings. Yet, when news of the crisis reached the public, it was the beleaguered "Goliath" that people were pulling for.

Similarly, despite the fact that two people in Seattle claimed to have found syringes in Diet Pepsi cans, it was Pepsi that the public overwhelmingly seemed to side with.

The Pepsi-Cola Company was confronted in 1993 with a case of either product-tampering or gross negligence at one or more of its bottling plants. It was not the first time someone claimed to have found some type of foreign object or matter in a beverage can. But a syringe—and two of them at that—seemed to tax credibility. Two days later, a third report came in from New Orleans. The company knew that in addition to a tampering problem, it had a major public relations problem to deal with.

Unlike Johnson & Johnson in the Tylenol matter, Pepsi refused to recall its product. A crisis team was assembled and one day later the president and CEO of Pepsi-Cola North America was appearing on network TV newscasts with an explanation and a videotape showing the Pepsi bottling process. The tape showed how cans are turned upside down and filled within seconds, thus leaving no room or time for foreign objects to be inserted and asserting that the claims made might be interesting, but they were also impossible to be achieved.

A commissioner with the U.S. Food and Drug Administration came forward, saying it was "simply not logical to conclude that a nationwide tampering has occurred based upon the large number of geographical locations of bottling plants, production dates that are months apart and the variety of products and containers involved.

"It is well known that even one report of possible tampering can—and will—lead to unfounded reports. Reports of possible tampering breed additional reports. It is a vicious cycle. That is what we believe happened here."

Two days later several people were arrested for filing false reports. Further, a surveillance video from a Colorado retailer showed a customer trying to force a syringe into an open Pepsi can. The video and report would seem to indicate that Pepsi had been not just the victim of a hoax, but a victim across the board. The reputation of both the company and the product had been put at risk. Some supermarkets and convenience stores briefly pulled Pepsi and Diet Pepsi from their shelves while product tampering charges were investigated.

Product tampering is a scary proposition. It holds that "any nut out there" can get at a product that has already undergone stringent quality control and safety procedures.

The reaction of Pepsi in this case shows how far some companies have come from the old system of issuing no comment while management panics.

Pepsi showed no arrogance or doubt about the integrity of its bottling and quality control process. The early appearance of the company's CEO on network TV, relaxed, confident, and willing to face questions from reporters, reassured customers and stockholders that the company's management was on top of the situation. The result was that customers' support of the product didn't waver. If anything, the public felt a degree of sympathy because someone was attempting to victimize the company to create a bogus charge of negligence and seek compensation. It was another case of Goliath proving to be a friendly giant.

When People Stopped Listening to What Used to Be E. F. Hutton

The most successful advertising campaign the company ever produced included a line that was the stuff copywriters' dreams are made of. It was one of those lines that would find its way into dinner conversations and comedians' monologues. The line was simply, "When E. F. Hutton talks, people listen."

E. F. Hutton was one of the most respected names on Wall Street. Indeed, it was one of only two or three brokerage firm names known even by people who had never owned a share of stock. Formed by Edward Francis Hutton in 1904, the firm drew considerable strength from its far-flung branch office system. As is often the case, big was synonymous with strong and secure, which was what nervous investors look for in someone to handle their money. Hutton fit the bill perfectly. Trust was the ultimate aim of a brokerage firm (after profit), and Hutton became one of the most trusted names in the business.

That made it all the more shocking when, on the threshold of 1988, E. F. Hutton ceased to exist. It was sold to American Express Company for $960 million. It would become the third name after the second slash in what would be Shearson/Lehman/Hutton-American Express, joining two other once-proud investment houses that had been crippled in later life.

Should investors care if E. F. Hutton is called Shearson, etc.?

Maybe not.

Should the brokerage or financial services industry even take note of yet another merger/acquisition/bailout?

Yes.

Both brokers and investors have always known the value of a "name" firm. In the financial services industry, a good name meant dignity, prestige, and stability. And more business. When an investor heard the caller was from Plumtree and Ashcan Associates, he or she rarely could find the time to talk, but let the caller be from Merrill Lynch, Paine Webber, or E. F. Hutton and people made time to listen. Brokers knew this. Jobs with the large, prestigious, multi-office wire-houses were coveted. They were the major league.

But the story of the fall of E. F. Hutton is more than a story of hard times and bad markets. Just as its sister American Express-owned firm Lehman Brothers' story was best summed up in the title of a fine book called *Greed and Glory on Wall Street,* the Hutton saga is well detailed in a volume titled appropriately *Sudden Death: The Rise and Fall of E. P. Hutton.*

Both firms were at the top of their class and were brought down not by the uncertainty of roller coaster markets **or** fickle investor preferences. Both firms can be said to have self-destructed, victims of greed, politics, and ego.

The beginning of the end for Hutton was a 1982 phone call to Hutton's legal department, wherein a New York State Banking Commission deputy superintendent wanted to inquire "about Hutton's banking practices."

The practices in question, since widely reported, had to do with a process called *chaining.*

It is also called *pinwheelmg.*

Most people know **it** as *check-kiting.* This **is** where uncleared checks are shifted from one bank account to another for the purpose of showing balances against which checks are written before the funds are actually available. If one moves fast enough ..and doesn't get caught, one can have use of money that technically does not exist. Obviously, the practice is illegal.

And E. F. Hutton got caught doing it.

As Mark Stevens writes in *Sudden Death,* "Hutton had clearly crossed the threshold of aggressive cash management and had forayed into the danger zone of corporate fraud. . . . Culpability for Hutton's fraudulent practices extended from the retail brokerage executives... to corporate headquarters,"

Hutton's leadership at the time believed that the best way to diffuse the scandal, the intense media scrutiny, and controversy was **to** attempt **to** plea-bargain the matter through the legal system quietly, a move that proved to be disastrous.

Unlike Johnson & Johnson, whose dignified handling of the Tylenol tragedy cost them more that $100 million for a recall it perhaps didn't have to do—and in a scandal for which it was not responsible—Hutton's agreeing to pay a fine of a comparably low $1 million only heightened its problems in that it represented a fine of $1,000 per count on 2,000 counts of fraud. About the best thing one might say about it is that at least no one died.

According to Mark Stevens, a Hutton executive commented, "Within hours of the guilty plea, swarms of reporters were over us like waves of killer bees. And why not? We gave them the story of a lifetime: 'Major Securities Firm Admits to 1,000 Counts of Fraud!'"

Supposedly the plea-bargain strategy was the result of endless consultation with lawyers, PR people, and the Hut-ton board. While it is reasonable to envision PR strategists suggesting that the firm be honest and take responsibility, the part that strains credibility is that most everyone then seemed to believe that upon admission of guilt and paying the fine, the problem would go away. An apology and an offer of restitution frequently will bring forgiveness, but never does it erase the memory of the deed. Further, one must take into account the nature of Hutton's business. This was not a publisher of magazines or a manufacturer of bottle caps. This was an investment management firm that relied on its customers and the general public's trust for its very existence.

By 1985 the firm was in a mess. Credibility was gone and brokers were interviewing for jobs at firms that they would have considered a step down just a year earlier.

Badly bleeding, ultimately the firm was sold.

Could E. F. Hutton have saved itself through a marketing solution?

It's questionable.

In a climate of greed and arrogance, where decisions are dominated by egos, marketing is only a part of the solution.

After the Nixon administration's Watergate scandal, one participant described his behavior as his having "lost his moral compass." That's a very dignified way to describe one's state after being caught in the commission of a crime. Plea-bargaining as an admission of guilt does not assure people whose money you would hope to handle that they can now trust you.

If Hutton was really interested in hanging on—in stabilizing its firm and rising again—for the sake of its customers, shareholders, employees, and the integrity of its industry, not just so senior management personnel could keep their jobs, it needed to travel a long way. Indications are that they were not prepared or willing to do so.

Mr. Stevens quotes a Hutton broker saying, "For years I'd gone to work each morning ready to take on the world, but that changed dramatically after the guilty plea. ... it looked like we were up to our eyeballs in crime. Clients believed that. Instead of managing their portfolios, I had to spend my time defending the company to people who'd trusted us for decades, for lifetimes. And no matter what I said, I couldn't convince everyone that the firm wasn't dishonest.

"On any given day, half the firm's brokers were on the phone giving their clients Button's side of the story. They weren't selling. They were spending their time explaining and defending and justifying. It was damage control on a massive scale and no one was getting paid for it."

People wondered why Hutton's management wasn't in jail. Hutton's business was built on trust and brokers were being told by people whose money they had managed for years that they couldn't be trusted anymore.

What might have been done?

Companies don't commit crimes, people commit crimes. Hutton should have demanded senior management's resignation, as well as the resignations of those with line responsibility for the transactions.

Senior management should have been replaced by individuals with impeccable credentials. After the collapse of Continental Bank in Chicago some years ago, the chairman of Amoco (Standard Oil Company) was lured out of retirement to assume at least interim control during reorganization. Similarly, Hutton could have tapped a retired governor, economist, or university president or lured from the bench a judge or other prominent figure to take the reins and restore customer, shareholder, and public confidence. What about a former chairman of the SEC or a retired commissioner?

Further, the Hutton board could have created a review board with people of high standing to act in an oversight capacity.

On the day of the plea bargain every Hutton client should have received a mailgram from the chairman of Hutton. It should have spelled out what had happened, why Hutton had chosen the course it had, and what was ahead for the firm. It should have requested understanding and support and made a pledge of maintaining an almost ninety-year tradition of integrity that had been only momentarily interrupted.

Like Johnson & Johnson's CEO, a Hutton designated

spokesperson, preferably the new CEO, should have gone public and made the rounds of the Sunday morning and late night TV news shows and offered interviews to the *New York Times* and the *Wall Street Journal*. These and other papers were already writing regularly on the Hutton scandal and, clearly, having felt betrayed, wanted some new bit of dirt each day if it was to be found. Having a spokesperson from senior management directly appeal to them for fairness and the use of their pulpit would at least somewhat mute the criticism that resulted from only press releases written by lawyers.

Paid television advertising that takes the firm's message right into people's living rooms might have helped. Instead of the very transparent TV commercials and print ads that used entertainer Bill Cosby as a spokesman, the new CEO of Hutton or a designated spokesperson should have told the audience, "Our firm's been through a rough period. That's behind us and we are looking to the future knowing we have to prove ourselves every day, and we are ready for that challenge. We ask that the public judge us by what we do from this day forward and we won't let you down ..."

Hutton could have published the message in advertorials and "open letter" ads and sent copies to every client, shareholder, and regulator.

Is this approach corny and just short of flag-waving?

Maybe.

Is it a lot better than hoping people have short memories and that "this too shall pass?"

Absolutely.

Alas, Hutton believed it had set up a good public relations program and "the matter would be history in a few weeks."

The public relations program was a disaster, short-sighted and ineffective. Within a year it was the firm itself that was history.

As a postscript to this case study, it is worth noting that 30 years after the scandal that brought down E.F. Hutton, a major financial crisis hit the United States and many of the leading financial organizations mentioned in this story, most notably Hutton's industry-leading rival, collapsed. The details will take years to sort out, but clearly indicate that throughout the financial services industry, a level of arrogance and elitism permeated the executive offices, causing industry leaders to believe they were so powerful nothing could stop them from doing whatever they wanted to do.

They were wrong.

First They Turned Green, Then Realistic

It seems like an unfortunate situation that would have a company's policy on environmental concerns be regarded as merely a business "trend" or, worse yet, a trend whose time has passed. Alas, as the twenty-first century begins, the trend may have ended.

The year was 1991. Society had evolved to a point where it could stand tall... and cough. The water was polluted, the air was polluted, there was a hole in Earth's ozone layer, and we were said to be, quite simply, killing ourselves with our very indulgent lifestyles. So, in the best tradition of American enterprise, having identified the problem and focused on it, it was time to begin marketing to it.

"Thanks to all of us, the planet is in trouble," wrote Joe Cappo in *Advertising Age,* "From the factory owner who spills poison into our drinking water, to the teenager who swills soda from a disposable bottle, to the primitive hunter who kills rhinoceroses, we are all guilty of contributing to the world's growing environmental problems.

"The funny thing about much of the environmental damage is that it has been accomplished while we were simply trying to do what human beings were supposed to do, improve our lives and make progress. Everything from the automobile to the disposable diaper was developed to make life better for the user . . . and to produce a profit for the manufacturer."

Mr. Cappo recognized the scope of the problem with more than an insightful editorial. In January 1991, *Advertising Age* published a special issue devoted solely to environmental marketing. Called "The Green Marketing Revolution," the forty-eight-page edition carried eleven separate environmental marketing articles and, just as significant in its way, some thirty ads, most of them full pages and all but two pitching their environmental connection. Note these headlines:

"The New Traditionalist. She wants much more than a clean house. She wants a cleaner world."

Good Housekeeping magazine

"Green Marketing Starts by Greening Your Own Backyard."

Rodale Press

"Our readers learn about the environment from some remarkable teachers."

National Geographic

"We wrote the book on environmentally friendly letterhead paper."

Crane & Company

"Scientific American's commitment to the environment is best illustrated through our own pages."

Scientific American magazine

"Our commitment to the environment is as old as the hills."

Times Mirror Magazines

Corporate America had been labeled the polluter and greedy predator of all natural resources, both animal and mineral. True, people seemed to like convenience foods and convenience packaging. It is also true that there are any number of enterprises that sustain themselves by creating causes and crises for which they can raise funds to create foundations and institutes and other lucrative endeavors in the name of a good cause. And who better to target as the cause of the problem than big business, that faceless, heartless, giant pillar of greed.

While this inference may seem cynical or suspicious, it's not without foundation. From human rights and pro-choice to gun control, causes today are big business in themselves. But each of these, and most other special interest causes, will not appeal to the vast majority of consumers, no matter how important the issue or how dreadful the disease. People whose lives haven't or might never be touched by violent crime, AIDS, or discrimination will be the most reluctant contributors and supporters.

But how does one say no to a plea to stop the destruction of the planet and the very air and water we need to stay alive? Astute organizers saw a potential gold mine here. Some may truly have been pure of mind and heart; others turned a problem into an opportunity.

And after decades of ignoring the petitions and pickets and low-impact boycotts, big business saw some things beginning to happen:

1. The crusades were beginning to have an effect. TV and newspapers began giving increasing coverage to the issues that not only hurt business, but left a negative residue that might well hurt future business and provide opportunities to competitors.
2. Legislators taking the pulse of consumers (constituents) might well see an opportunity to champion a cause at the expense of business.
3. Astute businesspeople saw an opportunity to change their black hats to white. They would take the side of the angels and become corporate sponsors in the quest to save the world.

More cynicism? Hardly.

Consider that 1970 saw the first commemoration of what its organizers named Earth Day. In their attempts to focus attention on problems and villains, the organizers were pretty much dismissed as kooks and hippies.

But twenty years later, Earth Day 1990 saw every celebrity in America and a host of corporations lining up to identify with the cause and show what noble corporate citizens they were. For some, the identification was so transparent as to be embarrassing.

For others, the link was genuine and, albeit defensive and belated, welcomed by consumers.

"You can fool some of the people all of the time . . . and that's enough to earn a decent living," environmentalist Denis Hayes wrote in *Advertising Age*. "Some ads tell a narrow truth, but a truth that is carefully calculated to mislead. . . . This year's hot cause is the environment. Whisky, overalls, toothpaste, shampoo, and myriad other products are being hawked with a public notice that a portion of any profits will go to save a remote rain forest or at least an environmental group that will accept the windfall."

Poor corporate America just can't get a break. There are always those who will question its motives and, based on past history, perhaps rightly so.

Sometimes taking a position or issuing a response isn't enough. It's not just you against the whole world, it is you against people who have put together a machine specifically for the purpose of taking you down. Furriers don't only have critics, they have anti-fur groups. Greenpeace, conceived and formed with the best intentions, often gets so mired in its agenda as to invite suspicion.

Bill Walker, a Greenpeace public relations person, writing in the organization's own magazine, told of attending a Public Relations Society of America convention in 1990, where the theme was "Our World in Transition." Mr. Walker's own assessment of the program caused him to view it as "How to Make Your Corporation Look Like a Friend to the Planet While Reaping a Billion in the International Waste Trade." Could anything anyone might have done have impressed Mr. Walker? It's doubtful. He had apparently not gone prepared to be impressed, but to find more subjects and companies to add to his hit list.

In fairness, some of the conference attendees not only played into his hands, but probably should have been in another line of work. Witness such direct quotes as "there are lots of reasons to feel sorry for Exxon," attributed to former NEC News president William Small. Three other pieces of advice from attendees: if people in the community hated ChemLawn for its manufacturing poisonous chemicals, change the company's name; if you let critics rant and rave, the community will sometimes get turned off and approach you with a compromise; you can short-circuit outside agitators by letting them disrupt public meetings so people become annoyed enough to want a private meeting with you.

Crisis marketing—crisis management—like the ongoing management of the business itself should be based on honesty, integrity, and on being a good corporate citizen. It is not based on a systematic plan to deceive the public. The very solid contribution of Greenpeace, anti-fur groups, and others in their position is to force business to rethink, revise, or, at least, have its position so well-justified that an attack alone doesn't change public opinion of them.

In an earlier section on "cause marketing," it was noted that the identification must be both sincere and a good fit or the effort will likely (and deservedly) backfire.

The term *green marketing* blossomed in the 1990s. Most major media not only report on it but have assigned specific reporters to the beat and, in many cases, created logos to identify the features.

"These days, good guys seem to be popping up all over," wrote Shelly Garcia in AD WEEK. "If Earth Day 1990 was the most visible sign of the greening of Corporate America, the months since have brought a stream of activities from companies trying to find their own greener pastures."

The first forum on "green" marketing was held in St. Paul, Minnesota, in March 1990. The exchanges were rather telling of things to come.

Minnesota's then-Attorney General Hubert H. Humphrey III told the gathering of nearly one hundred marketers and representatives of state and federal government and special interest groups that "the promise of this green revolution is too important to squander. But already it is at risk... from confusion... half-truths... innuendo and deception."

Advertising Age reported that phrases such as "environmentally friendly," "safe for the environment," "biodegradable," and "recyclable" presumably would require marketers to prove claims. The magazine noted that without federal standards and guidelines, however, products such as Glad plastic trash bags could carry the claim "safe for the environment" while simply meaning that the product will not harm the environment if it's placed in a landfill.

The director of the Federal Trade Commission (FTC) Bureau of Consumer Protection called upon private industry to establish environmental marketing guidelines and regulations.

Just two months later, *Advertising Age* executive editor Dennis Chase wrote "No previous 'movement' has ever been embraced by marketers this rapidly. Not the civil rights movement. Not the feminist movement. Not rock 'n' roll. Certainly not the first Earth Day twenty years ago, which caused barely a ripple among marketers. . . . But times have changed—especially for marketers."

In a September 1990 commentary in *Research* magazine under the headline "An Earthy Business: The Environmental Industry Cleans Up," Lynne Bennett noted, "Analysts predict that environmental companies will be prime beneficiaries of the public's increasing push to eliminate man-made poisons from the earth." The story went on to tell how public interest in "going green" had not only made good guys out of many bad guys, but presented great investment opportunities in the stock of companies that would likely play a major role in environmental cleanup. Buying stock in an environmental company is, in a sense, similar to investing in a company that makes bombs during wars, only it's much more of a "feel good" investment: you profit from environmental cleanup on two levels—a good return on your investment, while saving the world.

A 1991 *Good Housekeeping/Roper* survey showed 90 percent of the women surveyed described themselves as concerned about environmental issues. Yet, a study by the advertising agency Saatchi & Saatchi suggested "behavior has not caught up with attitudes… 16 percent or less of consumers act on their (environmental) concerns in terms of real behavior."

That figure, if true, really should not surprise marketers. It is one thing to identify a trend, but quite another to turn it into business. Traditionally, survey respondents will give the responses they believe their questioners are looking for. Most people watch a fair amount of television, but are uncomfortable admitting it. It's not a very intellectual pursuit. People tend to exaggerate the amount of time they exercise and downplay the amount of junk food they eat.

So Americans are pro-environment, except when it comes to actually doing something about it. This presents yet another opportunity for marketers. Take advantage of your market's desire to do something without actually making them do anything.

- Opt for pro-environmentally sound ingredients in products—non-polluting, recyclable, made from natural fibers, or similar components or ingredients.

- Contribute a portion of income to an environmental issue, such as solar energy, clean air, saving forests.

- Offer "feel good" premiums with your product, such as books or tapes on the environment, seeds, or plants.

Some companies have led the way in green marketing from the day they opened their doors. One such company, originally formed in Great Britain, is The Body Shop, a highly successful chain of health and beauty supply stores that carries its own line of environmentally safe products. Most all of their advertising is referral (word-of-mouth) and their loyal, worldwide constituency continues to grow.

Other companies, while perhaps late starters, made up for lost time by embracing pro-environment elements: Coca-Cola and Pepsi-Cola both expect to win a larger market share with recycled plastic bottles; Fuji film wants its film in paper canisters as opposed to plastic; McDonald's and Wendy's are large users of recycled paper for napkins and bags. Few companies, however, have made the leap from fast-food purveyor to white knight—or maybe that should be green knight—better than McDonald's. With an assist from the Environmental Defense Fund, in itself an excellent public relations move, McDonald's revamped so much of its operating style and packaging that *ADWEEK's Marketing Week* described Big Mac as repainting its golden arches green. Their program includes using brown carryout bags made from recycled paper, recycling cardboard boxes at each restaurant, serving coffee in washable mugs instead of paper cups, replacing single-serve ketchup packers with a pump dispenser, and some three dozen other changes thus moving on from the days of styrofoam burger packages and bleached paper bags.

All of the changes can't be transitioned in immediately, but it's a start. It is no small matter, nor is it subtle, that McDonald's would announce its program of "forty-two environmental initiatives," naming the Environmental Defense Fund as its advisor. It was a very impressive move.

Robert Glaser, president of Cleveland-based Ecomax, offers, "in green marketing, as in other advocacy efforts, the strategy must be used as a vehicle for total involvement, going beyond the current labeling and marketing campaigns. . . . Green marketing should begin from the ground up, in product development, not in the final marketing strategy. . . . Green marketing campaigns, in order to be truly legitimate rather than exploitive, must be built on long-term marketing advantages."

Maybe.

Certainly converts to the cause, such as McDonald's and Coca-Cola, weren't thinking of the environment at the product development stage and for years after it didn't seem at all necessary to pursue such thoughts. Both companies, however, took the pulse of their constituency and responded, making it easy for their customers to feel good about using their products.

Fortune magazine, in a cover story titled "The Environment: Business joins the New Crusade," offered, "Trend spotters and forward thinkers agree that the Nineties will be the Earth Decade and that environmentalism will be a movement of massive worldwide force." The article cites DuPont, 3M, Procter & Gamble, and McDonald's as being among the nation's "smartest companies" for understanding the public tilt toward environmentalism and supporting the effort at a cost of hundreds of millions of dollars.

Yet, if the cause is such an obvious and righteous one, there are nonetheless cynics. The public is keenly aware that noble causes that rate magazine cover stories and TV specials are ultimately short-lived.

Is environmentalism and green marketing merely a very hot trend to set the tone for a new business order? Some people allow for the possibility.

Advertising Age held the first "Green Marketing Summit Conference" in New York in early 1991. The magazine reported that "an unusual spirit of cooperation was evident among the attending government officials, environmental groups and private companies. And yet there was an unmistakable wariness. Environmental advocates could not quell suspicions about business motives, fearing that companies are thinking 'green' only in terms of 'long green,' rather than the environment. To take a leading role, marketers must demonstrate an honest and open effort to meet the public's demand for products and services that support the world we all inhabit."

Robert Barrett, general manager, solid waste management solutions group for Mobil Chemical Company, noted that Mobil had "concluded that biodegradable plastics will not help solve the solid waste problem. . . . We do, however, see that there are some short-term public relations gains to switching to a photo-degradable plastic grocery sack or consumer trash bag, or even a biodegradable bag of each type. And it's that public relations value that has to be considered as opposed to real solutions to the problem."

Mobil's vice president for marketing and sales, David Marshall, added, "Faced with consumer demand, regulatory situations, trade demands, and competitive offerings, we made the decision that we had to offer a degradable product to survive in the marketplace."

Public relations value and survival in the marketplace are two simple perspectives on responding to the new challenges with marketing solutions for a public that determines a company is doing well when it is doing good.

Wal-Mart Stores tag shelves to highlight products and packages that are environmentally friendly. The chain's vice president of marketing and sales promotion, Paul Higham, notes: "Ours is not a marketing ploy. We really are committed. . . . We don't see this as a marketing issue. We see this as the sort of thing we need to do as good citizens of our country and this planet."

Is, then, green marketing the future or the response of corporations under fire? The answer is both. Being a "good corporate citizen" is good business. People who use your products or are your clients want to be reassured that they made the right choices.

Reassure them with honesty, directness, and every possible effort to represent yourself as a good neighbor.

"Some companies have taken the time to do it right," says Green Seal, Inc., chairman Denis Hayes. "They make products that are elegant, durable, repairable and, eventually, recyclable. . . . They are what true green consumerism is all about."

This could get tricky here. Mr. Hayes, the originator of Earth Day, the head of "Green Seal," and a newspaper columnist, seeks to create a certification program for companies that are truly serious about environmental friendliness. While the spirit of the movement might be in his favor, actual acquiescence from business is another matter. It took many years for the "Good Housekeeping Seal" to have any serious marketing value. Hayes and Green Seal might believe their standards are realistic enough to invite corporate cooperation, but then the same might have been said for the Environmental Protection Agency (EPA) standards. That agency had virtually evolved into being the pollution police.

If history is our example, corporations who see value in getting certified with a green seal (just perhaps not Mr. Hayes's Green Seal) will likely simply set up a competing accrediting group. Ted Brenner, president of the Soap and Detergent Association, a home products trade group, told *ADWEEK,* "We're not blackballing the seal programs. It's not our business, but if we think there are better ways to approach the problem, it's incumbent upon us to do it."

Perhaps everyone will fall into step behind Green Seal, then again...

Times changed. A 1996 *Newsweek* story noted "Eco-labels aren't big in America, where only a handful of items bear the imprimatur of Green Seal, Inc., or the cross and globe of its competitor, Scientific Certification Systems." The story offered that green consumerism is big throughout much of Europe, but quotes a Procter & Gamble spokesman as saying, "Eco-Seals potentially create trade barriers." That is to suggest a lack of uniform regulation around the world keeps global companies from participating in international green marketing efforts.

People who laughed at the idea not many years ago are now part of the mainstream, recognizing that recycling is an important contribution to saving the planet. Otherwise well-mannered people openly, often rudely, call attention to those who pollute and litter.

Noble crusades tend to be cyclical in marketing: red meat is a prime source of protein and the main dish in a healthy diet, then red meat is out for health reasons, then back in again. The same can be said of dairy products and aggressive campaigns to fight poverty and hunger. They are all noble causes, embraced by business in the interest of making a contribution to our cities, towns, and most worthy causes.

But as so much of marketing is geared toward the current campaign, issues and causes come and go. During tough seasons—which seem to be most times—the Inevitable large budget cuts require that saving the world is often deferred. This can be a mistake. In building the reservoir of goodwill, so necessary to draw upon in a crisis situation, a long and continuous record of green marketing can be extremely valuable.

Ecology became environmentalism and in the twenty-first century it will probably be called something else . . . and be gone from the front page. But it will more than likely be a simple fact of everyday life.

The first celebration of Earth Day took place in 1970. From that beginning came the Earth Day Network (EDN), a driving force steering environmental awareness around the world with an international network of more than 17,000 organizations in 174 countries. Its domestic programs engage 5,000 groups and over 25,000 educators coordinating millions of community development and environmental protection activities throughout the year. More than a billion people participate in Earth Day each year. It is the only event celebrated simultaneously around the globe by people of all backgrounds, faiths and nationalities.

Appendix

Sources and Resources

Marketing people tend to be very proud of what they do. Just as advertising and public relations are considered the "glamorous" areas, where creativity shines and celebrities abound, the marketing people are usually the ones with the senior titles, MBAs, and overall budget responsibilities. In a manner of speaking, the marketing people often represent the strategic and business side of the creative arts in the profession. So when unpleasant substances, usually of a waste-like nature, begin to hit the proverbial fan—the crisis—it is usually the lawyers and marketers who, while not always agreeing on the approach, pull together to protect the corporate franchise.

The lawyers use the law and the marketers use whatever else is available. Their objectives are to capitalize on the past history, reputation, brand loyalty, goodwill, and quality of the corporation's products, services, and people. All's fair. Appeal to the public's emotions, fairness, greed, sympathy, and empathy.

Like their legal brethren, marketers often turn to their notebooks to arm themselves for battle. Here are some of the better ones.

Magazines

Advertising Age. Published weekly by Crain Communications, 740 N. Rush Street, Chicago, IL 60611-2.590. Yes, the name says advertising, but this is indispensable reading for anyone whose work is marketing. *Advertising Age* has grown from an agency trade journal to a weekly overview of national and global news, trends, and economics. Upfront stories often present an analysis of how the week's major news affects marketers. Special pull-out sections on media and creativity have become "keepers" and occasionally, as with special issues on such topics as "The Green Marketing Revolution," staples of corporate, agency, and consultant reference libraries. Despite the occasional "makeover" of the publication that attempts to give it a fresh, contemporary look, but somewhat confuses the old-timers, columns by Rance Crain, James Brady, and Joe Cappo offer the pulse of the industry.

ADWEEK. Published fifty-one times a year by ASM Communications, 1515 Broadway, New York, NY 10036. A weekly newspaper in magazine form, it provides a solid file on advertising and marketing. News is fresh, substantive, and informative. Columns by Mark Dolliver are bright and Bji-bara Lippert's writing and insight are often worth the price of the magazine alone.

Marketing News. Published biweekly by the Publications Group of the American Marketing Association, Suite 200, 150 S. Wacker Drive, Chicago, IL 60606-5819. Neatly segmented regular features and columns on Event Marketing, Education, Ethics, Sports, and Perspectives on a wide range of subjects. This publication has a classy way of taking a "marketing lesson" and imparting it gently.

Marketing Management. Published quarterly by the Publications Group of the American Marketing Association, Suite 200, 250 S. Wacker Drive, Chicago, IL 60606-5819. Very useful and very upscale "coffee table" magazine with departments such as

Marketing Law, Marketing Briefs, Marketing Masters, and longer in-depth feature stories.

American Demographics. A monthly publication of Dow-Jones & Co., American Demographics, Inc., 127 W. State Street, Ithaca, NY 14850. A serious magazine aimed largely at market researchers, but extremely useful to virtually everyone else in the agency or marketing department. It is contemporary, bright, stylish, and packed with a broad range of marketing-oriented pieces and special editions focusing on market segments, such as ethnic markets, seniors, and women.

Marketing Tools. Published eight times a year by American Demographics, 127 W. State Street, Ithaca, NY 14850. A relatively young publication that takes a "how-to" approach to subjects. Regular features on positioning, on-line, and database/direct marketing, to name only a few. This is an excellent companion publication to *American Demographics,* but is a solid stand-alone.

Sales & Marketing Management. Published monthly by Bill Communications, 355 Park Avenue, New York, NY 10010. Regular sections include Marketing Closeup, Technology Update, Leading Edge, Travel & Entertainment. How important can a marketing magazine be? One issue alone had articles by Arthur Miller, John Naisbitt, and Al Ries. It's mainstream business news with an edge.

The *Wall Street Journal.* Published daily, except Saturday, Sunday, and holidays by Dow-Jones & Co., New York. When the Journal went to three sections in the late 19803, many lamented the format-tampering. However, a benefit came in the form of section two: "Marketplace," a daily overview of top marketing, advertising, broadcast, cable, and print industry news with special columns devoted to legal and technology aspects of the major marketing-related stories. Serious marketers should be embarrassed if not reading it.

Books

Lesly's Handbook of Public Relations and Communications (Fifth edition), Philip Lesly, editor, NTC/Contemporary Publishing Company, 1998.

MaxiMarketing, Stan Rapp and Tom Collins, McGraw-HiU Book Company, 1987.

American Renaissance: Our Life at the Turn of the 21st Century, Marvin Cetron and Owen Davies, St. Martin's Press, 1989.

When the Bottom Drops: How Any Business Can Survive in the Coming Hard Times, A. David Silver, Prima Publishing and Communications, 1988.

Getting It Right the Second Time, Michael Gershman, Addi-son-Wesley Publishing Company, Inc., 1990.

FutureScope: Success Strategies for the 1990s *and Beyond,* Joe Cappo, Longman Financial Services/Dearborn Publishing, 1990.

The Marketer's Guide to Public Relations: How Today's Top Companies Are Using PR to Gain a Competitive Edge, Thomas L. Harris, John Wiley & Sons, Inc., 1991.

We're So Big and Powerful Nothing Bad Can Happen to Us: An Investigation of America's Crisis-Prone Corporations, Ian J. Mitroff and Thierry Pauchant, Birch Lane Press/ Carol Publishing, 1990.

Positioning: The Battle for Your Mind, Al Ries and Jack Trout, McGraw-Hill, Inc., 1981 and 1986. (Also published in paperback by Warner Books.)